Who Next...?

a guide to children's authors

2nd Edition

Edited by Norah Irvin

LISU Library & Information Statistics Unit

Loughborough University

IRVIN, Norah, Editor
Who Next...? A guide to children's authors

First published 1999, 2nd edition 2003
ISBN 1 901786 56 0

© LISU 2003

5820.99282

Cover design by
Kathryn Knapman, Media Services, Loughborough University
using reproductions from original cover images as follows:

Greedy Guts and Belly Busters by Rose Impey
Mona the Vampire books by Sonia Holleyman and Hiawyn Oram
Pet Pals *Noah and Nelly* by Geraldine McCaughrean
The Fire Within and *The Salt Pirates of Skegness* by Chris d'Lacey
Little Horrors *The Pumpkin Man* by Shoo Rayner
Stargirl by Jerry Spinelli
What Howls at the Moon in Frilly Knickers? by E F Smith
What Planet are you from Clarice Bean? by Lauren Child
courtesy of Orchard Books

Simone's Diary by Helena Pielichaty, illustrated by Sue Heap - this edition published April 2003
The Kite Rider by Geraldine McCaughrean - published March 2001
reproduced by permission of Oxford University Press

The Boggart and the Monster by Susan Cooper
The Other Side of Truth by Beverley Naidoo
by permission of Puffin Books

The Firework-maker's Daughter by Philip Pullman
Lizzie Zipmouth by Jacqueline Wilson, illustrated by Nick Sharratt
Up on Cloud Nine by Anne Fine
Voices in the Park by Anthony Browne
by permission of Random House Children's Books

Cover illustration © 1995 P J Lynch from *The Christmas Miracle of Jonathan Toomey*
    written by Susan Wojciechowski
Cover illustration © 1999 Brita Granström from *Eyes, Nose, Fingers and Toes*
    written by Judy Hindley
Cover illustration © 1997 Anthony Lewis from *The Owl Tree* written by Jenny Nimmo
Cover illustration and silhouette © 2000 Walker Books Ltd taken from *Stormbreaker*
    written by Anthony Horowitz
all reproduced by permission of Walker Books Ltd, London

Printed by
W & G Baird Ltd, Greystone Press, Antrim, N Ireland BT41 2RS

Published and distributed by
Library & Information Statistics Unit (LISU)
Loughborough University, Loughborough, LE11 3TU
Tel: +44 (0)1509 223071 Fax: +44 (0)1509 223072 E-mail: lisu@lboro.ac.uk
Web: www.lboro.ac.uk/departments/dis/lisu/lisuhp.html

Lesley Cooper

When the idea of creating a guide to children's fiction reading first emerged LISU was very fortunate to enlist two very knowledgeable and industrious enthusiasts as editors - Norah Irvin and Lesley Cooper. The outcome of their endeavours became clear as *Who Next?* exceeded expectations and drew universal praise. When we began thinking about the new edition of *Who Next?* we naturally expected to work with both of them again. Sadly it was not to be; some months into the preliminary stages of shaping the second edition, Lesley's life was cruelly cut short after a brave series of battles with cancer.

LISU lost an important contributor, Norah a valued collaborator and friend and on a personal level, I lost not only a valued professional colleague, but also a long-standing friend, since we had been students together at Loughborough many years ago. Things had come full circle with Lesley and me involved in the same project based at Loughborough.

Many tributes were paid at Lesley's memorial service to her courage and fortitude as well as to her commitment, integrity, approachability, helpfulness and passion for bringing children and books together.

All of us who have had anything to do with this edition are unanimous in our determination to make it a fitting memorial to Lesley. We hope that we live up to her example.

J Eric Davies - Director LISU

Contents

Acknowledgements

As with the first edition I owe a huge debt of thanks to many people without whose help this guide could not have been compiled. More so, this time, because tragically Lesley Cooper, my co-editor, died just after we started work on this edition. I have missed her extensive knowledge and the sheer pleasure of working with her very much. She was a very special person. I have very much appreciated the continued support of her family, especially her husband, Tony.

I have relied heavily again on the expertise and detailed knowledge of Sue Adler and Pam Dix of Islington Education Library Service (14-16 section) and Teresa Gibb of Hertfordshire Library Service (5-7 section) all of whom helped with the first edition.

I am especially grateful to Sue Jones together with Lesley Cooper's and my colleagues from Hertfordshire Schools' Library Service, who have given me constant help and encouragement.

The ideas and imagination of the many people who have contributed have helped to provide a broader scope and I would like to thank the following:

Lynne Hamer	Bath Children's Library - Bath & N E Somerset
Eileen McAllister	Bexley Grammar School
Megan Nelhams	Cape Cornwall School
Eileen Armstrong	Cramlington High School, Northumberland
Catriona Prynne	Dulwich Prep School, Cranbrook (DCPS), Kent
Shona Donaldson/Stuart Syme	Dundee City Council
Avo Kurvits	East Riding of Yorkshire Council
Brenda Rowan	Edinburgh City Libraries and Information Services
Beverley Van Holby	Essex County Council/Mayflower High School
Barbara Band	Fort Hill Community School, Hampshire
Clare Wooldridge	Haberdashers' Aske's Hatcham College
Claire Haslem	Maidstone Grammar School, Kent
Dorne Fraser	Norfolk Library & Information Service
Colin Brabazon	North Lincolnshire Libraries and Information Services
Eileen Castle	Perse Preparatory School, Cambridge
Sally Ballard	Ranelagh School, Bracknell Forest
Linda Riley	Sandbach Boys School, Cheshire
Helen Boothroyd & her team	Suffolk Children's and Schools Library Services
Janice Lavigueur	Trinity & All Saints University College, Horseforth, Leeds
Susan Deering-Punshon	West Berkshire CC
Susan Heyes	West Sussex Schools Library Service
Mary Bryning	Wirral Schools Library Service
Moira Arthur & Claire Duncombe	Peters Bookselling Services, Birmingham
Booktrust, London	

ii

Acknowledgements (cont)

I would like to thank Orchard Books, Oxford University Press, Puffin Books, Random House Children's Books and Walker Books Ltd, London for permission to incorporate reproductions of their jacket designs on the cover.

I am also grateful to my publisher Eric Davies, Director of LISU, for his help and support, and also to his colleagues Mary Ashworth and Sharon Fletcher, for their unfailing patience and help in providing a telephone hotline for any problems I encountered, for designing and typesetting the layout, and for developing the FilemakerPro database used in organising the content.

Finally, one of the best resources, my family: Brian Irvin a.k.a. Director of Communications!! and Rebecca Green and Simon Irvin for their data skills help.

Norah Irvin
Stevenage

Introduction

Who Next? A guide to children's authors is designed as a tool to help parents, teachers and librarians in schools and public libraries to guide children who have already enjoyed stories by one writer to find other authors they will enjoy reading.

The book lists 436 writers of children's fiction, and with each name suggests other authors who write in a similar way. The idea is that you look up one of your favourite children's authors, then try reading a book by one of the other authors listed underneath. By moving from one entry to another readers can expand the number of writers they enjoy. The same system has been used successfully in a similar guide to adult fiction. Also published by LISU, *Who Else Writes Like...? A reader's guide to fiction authors* is now in its fourth edition.

The links that have been made between authors are of genre and theme, and also of styles of writing, or similar aspects of characterisation and settings. Of course no author writes exactly like another and readers will not agree with all the choices. Questioning *Who Next?* may be one of the pleasures of using it, and a source for discussion and debate.

Most of the authors listed have written several books. I have tried to include books that are easily available, so you should be able to find the titles recommended in either a library or from a bookshop. Whilst recognising their importance in encouraging the love of reading, it was decided to exclude picture books for younger readers as the aim is to focus on the story rather than illustration. However, in response to suggestions from our users I have included a separate listing of 142 picture books suitable for older readers with very general guidance on theme. They are mostly multi-layered and can be used creatively to encourage and develop reading and language and for fun! Graphic novels are outside the scope of this listing but information on an excellent guide is included in the bibliography. Books written primarily for adults have not been included.

Who Next? is arranged by three 'audience age groups': children aged 5-7, 8-11 and 12-14. Where an author writes for more than one age group, this is shown. I have not attempted to define age ranges exactly as this is limiting, and my aim is to encourage children to read as widely as possible. I ask users of *Who Next?* to bear in mind the preferences, abilities and needs of individual children.

I have also included in the text a selection of titles for each author so that readers trying an author new to them have some idea of where to start.

At the end of *Who Next?* are indexes of authors by theme or genre and children's series, and a list of authors who have won prizes for their children's fiction.

I very much hope that the book will help many readers to enjoy more children's books. The intention is to produce a further edition in three years time, so if there are any names you think should be included (or you disagree strongly with any of the recommendations made), please do let my publisher, LISU, know.

Norah Irvin
Stevenage

How to Use This Guide

Author Lists

We have arranged the lists of authors by age range then alphabetically by author surname.

So, to use *Who Next?*, first select the appropriate age range, 5–7, 8–11 or 12–14. Then, in the alphabetical list, locate the author you want to match. There you will find the suggested alternative authors.

For example, a reader who is 9 years old and who likes Terence Blacker books might also enjoy stories by Neil Arksey, Bernard Ashley, Tony Bradman, Rob Childs, Michael Coleman, Alan Durant, Alan Gibbons, Michael Hardcastle, Kate Saunders or Martin Waddell.

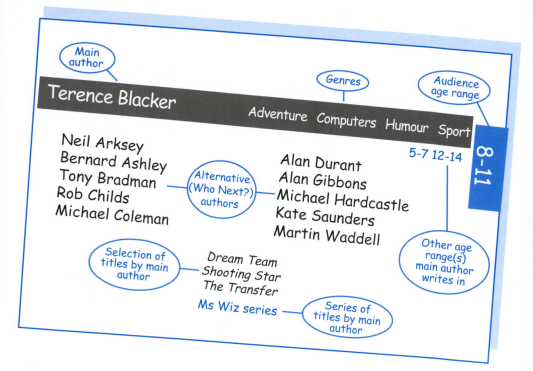

Main author

Genres

Audience age range

Terence Blacker

Adventure Computers Humour Sport

Neil Arksey
Bernard Ashley
Tony Bradman
Rob Childs
Michael Coleman

Alternative (Who Next?) authors

Alan Durant
Alan Gibbons
Michael Hardcastle
Kate Saunders
Martin Waddell

5-7 12-14

8-11

Other age range(s) main author writes in

Selection of titles by main author

Dream Team
Shooting Star
The Transfer

Ms Wiz series

Series of titles by main author

Where an author writes in a theme or genre, this is indicated. Do remember that some authors who frequently write in a particular category or for a specific age group sometimes produce a book in a quite different genre or for another age group. You can check this by reading the jacket details and summaries on the books themselves.

Picture Books for Older Readers

A new section to this edition is a selection of Picture Books for Older Readers on pages 157-164. These books are listed separately from the main sequence because the importance here is on the illustration and the story equally and this does not lend itself to *Who Next?* like comparisons.

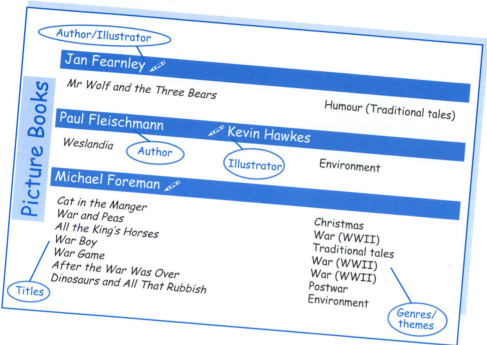

Genres and Themes

If you only want a list of authors who write in a particular category or genre, such as Adventure or Animals, then turn straight to the Genre lists which start on page 165.

Series

We have included a list of children's series starting on page 183. Many children's books are published within series and this is often a helpful guide to finding similar authors.

Current Children's Book Prizes

Books which have been awarded a special prize are listed on pages 187-196.

We believe you will find this guide easy to use but please remember, it is not infallible. Finally, if you do need more information, ask. Library and bookshop staff are very willing to help.

Allan Ahlberg

Animals   Family   Humour

8-11

John Cunliffe
Chris d'Lacey
P D Eastman
Vivian French
Anita Jeram

Theo Le Sieg
Colin McNaughton
Shoo Rayner
Dr Seuss
Pat Thomson

Fast Fox Goes Crazy
The Man Who Wore All His Clothes
Ms Cliff the Climber
Skeleton Crew

Eleanor Allen

Ghost/supernatural

Judy Allen
Andrew Donkin
Sarah Garland
Sam Godwin

Anthony Masters
Barbara Mitchelhill
Catherine Sefton
Theresa Tomlinson

Enter at Your Peril
Ghost from the Sea
Ghost on the Landing

Jonathan Allen

Humour   Magic

Terence Blacker
Humphrey Carpenter
Jonathan Emmett
Ann Jungman

Jill Murphy
Shoo Rayner
Michael Rosen

And Pigs Might Fly
King of the Birds
Wizard Grimweed Series

Don't forget: Picture Books * Genres * Series * Book Prizes * Bibliography ☞

1

Judy Allen — Animals Ghost/supernatural Humour

12-14

Eleanor Allen
Jane Gardam
Sarah Garland
Mary Hooper
Dick King-Smith

Brian Patten
Margaret Ryan
Angie Sage
Dyan Sheldon
Martin Waddell

Auntie Billie's Greatest Invention
Five Weird Days at Aunt Carly's
The Great Pig Sprint

Rachel Anderson — Family Friends

8-11 12-14

Claire Bevan
Helen Dunmore
Jamila Gavin

Penelope Lively
Jan Mark
Ann Pilling

Best Friends
Jessy Runs Away

Scoular Anderson — Ghost/supernat Historical Humour Magic

Tony Bradman
Mick Gowar
Julia Jarman
Jan Page
Frank Rodgers

Dee Shulman
Wendy Smith
Paul Stewart
Pat Thomson
Philip Wooderson

The Bin Bears
Ghost Docs at School
Rob the Roman Gets Eaten by a Lion (Nearly)
Wizard's Boy Series

Don't forget: Picture Books * Genres * Series * Book Prizes * Bibliography ☞

Laurence Anholt

Humour

8-11

Adrian Boote
Herbie Brennan
Keith Brumpton
Roald Dahl
Rose Impey

Robert Leeson
Andrew Matthews
Tony Mitton
Bob Wilson

Eco-Wolf and the Three Pigs
Mickey the Muckiest Boy
Shampoozel
Tina the Tiniest Girl

Roy Apps

Adventure   Historical   Humour   Magic

8-11

Tony Bradman
Humphrey Carpenter
Jonathan Emmett
Philippa Gregory
Dennis Hamley

Julia Jarman
Ann Jungman
Kaye Umansky
Karen Wallace

A Camp to Hide King Alfred
Chimney Charlie
Frankie Stein's Robot
Nigel and the Pirate

Twitches Series

Phyllis Arkle

Adventure   Animals

Henrietta Branford
Peter Clover
Jenny Dale
Elizabeth Hawkins
Tessa Krailing

Hiawyn Oram
K M Peyton
Jill Tomlinson
Colin West

The Railway Cat
The Railway Cat and the Horse
The Railway Cat's Secret

Elizabeth Arnold
Family   Friends   Humour

Lisa Bruce
Sheila Lavelle
Hilary McKay

Ann Pilling
Emily Smith

Scraggy Flies High
Thief in the Garden
The Triple Trouble Gang

Brian Ball
Animals   Family   Friends

Harriet Castor
June Crebbin
Adèle Geras
Rose Impey
Andrew and Paula Martyr

Kara May
Hilda Offen
Daniel Postgate
Angie Sage
Wendy Smith

Bella at the Ballet
Hop It, Duggy Dog!
Thank You, Duggy Dog!

Antonia Barber
Ballet   Friends

Adèle Geras
Angela Kanter

Jean Ure

Best Foot Forward
Dance to the Rescue
In the Wings
Lucy's Next Step
Model Dancers

Alan Baron
Animals   Humour

Judy Hindley
Rose Impey
Anita Jeram

Jillian Powell
Phyllis Root
Colin West

Little Pig's Bouncy Ball
Red Fox and the Baby Bunnies
The Red Fox Monster

Stan and Jan Berenstain 5-7

Humour

Bennett Cerf
P D Eastman
Anita Jeram
Theo Le Sieg

Hilary Robinson
Dr Seuss
Colin West

Berenstain Bears on the Moon
Berenstain Bears on Wheels
C is for Clown

Claire Bevan

Family   Humour

Rachel Anderson
Helen Dunmore
Jamila Gavin

Jan Mark
Ann Pilling

Lucky Numbers
Make 'em Laugh
The Shoe Box Millionaire

Terence Blacker

Humour   Magic   School

8-11 12-14

Jonathan Allen
Humphrey Carpenter

Ann Jungman
Jill Murphy

Ms Wiz and the Sister of Doom
Ms Wiz Goes to Hollywood
Ms Wiz Smells a Rat

Malorie Blackman   Adventure   Magic   Other lands   Sci fiction

8-11 12-14

Lisa Bruce
Ann Cameron
Jamila Gavin

Douglas Hill
Julia Jarman

The Monster Crisp Guzzler
Snow Dog
Space Race
Whizziwig

Betsey Biggelow Series

Jon Blake

Adventure   Family   War 1939-45

Sarah Garland
Dennis Hamley
Sam McBratney
Colin McNaughton

Brian Patten
Dyan Sheldon
Alexander McCall Smith

Danger Eyes
Litttle Stupendo Flies High
The Sandbag Secret

Adrian Boote

Adventure   Fantasy   Humour

Laurence Anholt
Keith Brumpton
Roald Dahl

Jonathan Emmett
Jeremy Strong

The Ice Cream Cowboys
The Lemonade Genie
The Lollipop Knight
Madcap Moonwood
The Strawberry Sorcerer

Tony Bradman

Fantasy   Ghost/supernatural   Humour

8-11

Scoular Anderson
Roy Apps
Marc Brown
Damon Burnard
Chris d'Lacey

Roald Dahl
Tessa Krailing
Marilyn McLaughlin
Margaret Nash
Selina Young

Dilly the Dinosaur
Dilly and the School Play
The Ghost Teacher
The Magnificent Mummies
Midnight in Memphis

Don't forget: Picture Books * Genres * Series * Book Prizes * Bibliography ☞

Henrietta Branford

Adventure   Animals   Fantasy

8-11 12-14

5-7

Phyllis Arkle
Peter Clover
Helen Cresswell
Pippa Goodhart

Philippa Gregory
Elizabeth Hawkins
Jill Tomlinson

Dimanche Diller at Sea
Dimanche Diller in Danger
Royal Blunder
Royal Blunder and the Haunted House

Herbie Brennan

Adventure   Detective mysteries   Humour

8-11

Laurence Anholt
Roald Dahl

Robert Leeson

Eddie the Duck
Eddie and the Dirty Dogs
Zartog's Remote

Theresa Breslin

Family   Humour   School

8-11 12-14

Keith Brumpton
Anne Fine
Sarah Garland
Mick Gowar
Joan Lingard

Hilary McKay
Jan Mark
Jenny Nimmo
Jacqueline Wilson

Blair the Winner
Name Games

Joyce Lancaster Brisley

Family   Humour

Dorothy Edwards

Bel Mooney

Milly Molly Mandy Stories

Jeff Brown — Adventure   Fantasy

Susan Gates
Douglas Hill
Sam McBratney

Alf Prøysen
Alexander McCall Smith
Jeremy Strong

Flat Stanley
Invisible Stanley
Stanley's Christmas Adventure

Marc Brown — Animals   Family   Friends   Humour

Tony Bradman
Damon Burnard
James Marshall
Chris Powling

Frank Rodgers
Dr Seuss
Francesca Simon
Ian Whybrow

DW in Trouble
Wings on Things
Arthur Series

Lisa Bruce — Adventure   Friends   Other cultures

Elizabeth Arnold
Malorie Blackman
Ann Cameron
Jamila Gavin
Mary Hoffman

Geraldine McCaughrean
Hilda Offen
Hiawyn Oram
Karen Wallace

Dynamite Deela: School Trouble
Dynamite Deela: Trouble for Deela
Jazeera in the Sun
Jazeera's Journey
Nani's Holiday

Don't forget: Picture Books ∗ Genres ∗ Series ∗ Book Prizes ∗ Bibliography ☞

Keith Brumpton

Fantasy   Historical   Humour

Laurence Anholt
Adrian Boote
Theresa Breslin
Roald Dahl
Mick Gowar

Douglas Hill
Sam McBratney
Jeremy Strong
Martin Waddell

Chariots on Fire!
Superheroes Down the Plughole
The Sword in the Scone

Janet Burchett and Sarah Vogler

Humour   Sport

Rob Childs
Michael Coleman
Alan Durant

Martin Waddell
Bob Wilson

The Cup Final
Ghost Striker
Tigers on Telly

Damon Burnard

Adventure   Humour

Tony Bradman
Marc Brown
Vivian French

Paul Stewart
Pat Thomson
Ian Whybrow

Bullysaurus and the Alien
Bullysaurus Under the Sea
Danny Longlegs
Zebedee Zing, Taster to the King

Ann Cameron

Family   Friends   Humour

Malorie Blackman
Lisa Bruce
Dorothy Edwards
Jamila Gavin

Julia Jarman
Francesca Simon
Alexander McCall Smith
Emily Smith

Banana Spaghetti
Huey's Tiger
Julian Series

Lindsay Camp
Animals   Sport

June Crebbin

Shoo Rayner

Sam and Mr Wallace
Sammy's Super Season

Humphrey Carpenter
Humour   Magic   School

Jonathan Allen
Roy Apps
Terence Blacker

Andrew Matthews
Jill Murphy
Kaye Umansky

Mr Majeika
Mr Majeika and the Ghost Train
Mr Majeika and the School Book Week
Mr Majeika Vanishes

Anne Cassidy
Animals   Humour

Penny Dolan
Maggie Moore
Margaret Nash
Jillian Powell

Alison Ritchie
Hilary Robinson
Barry Wade

The Cheeky Monkey
The Crying Princess
Pippa and Poppa

Harriet Castor
Animals   Ballet   Friends

Brian Ball
Adèle Geras
Penelope Lively
Alan MacDonald

Alison Prince
Shoo Rayner
Catherine Sefton

Ballet Magic
Ballet Magic on Stage
Fat Puss and Friends

Bennett Cerf

5-7

Humour

Stan and Jan Berenstain
P D Eastman

Theo Le Sieg
Dr Seuss

Book of Animal Riddles
Book of Riddles
More Riddles

Simon Cheshire

Adventure   Friends   Humour

8-11

Mary Hooper
Sam McBratney
Dyan Sheldon
Francesca Simon

Ian Whybrow
David Henry Wilson
Jacqueline Wilson

Me and My Big Mouse

Rob Childs

Historical   School   Sport

8-11

Janet Burchett and
     Sarah Vogler
Michael Coleman

Alan Durant
Bob Wilson

The Big Clash
The Big Send Off
Great Hit
Remember, Remember the Fifth of November
Wicked Day

Pomme Clayton

Mythology

Margaret Mahy
Margaret Mayo

Geraldine McCaughrean

The Girl With Golden Fingers
The Girl Who Married a Bear
The Girl Who Went to the Underworld

Peter Clover — Adventure Animals Pony/horse

Phyllis Arkle
Henrietta Branford
Jenny Dale
Lucy Daniels
Jane Gardam

Elizabeth Hawkins
Dick King-Smith
Hiawyn Oram
K M Peyton
Jill Tomlinson

Donkey Diaries
Hercules
Rescue Riders
Sheltie Series

Michael Coleman — Friends Humour School Sport

Janet Burchett and
   Sarah Vogler
Rob Childs
Gillian Cross
Alan Durant

Mary Hooper
Geraldine McCaughrean
Martin Waddell
Karen Wallace
Bob Wilson

Fizzy in the Spotlight
Angels FC Series

June Crebbin — Fantasy Ghost/supernatural Humour

Brian Ball
Lindsay Camp
Roald Dahl
Alan Durant
Jan Fearnley

Anne Fine
Penelope Lively
Nick Sharratt
Martin Waddell

The Curse of the Skull
Dinnertime Rhyme
Emmeline and the Monster
No Tights for George

Don't forget: Picture Books * Genres * Series * Book Prizes * Bibliography ☞

Helen Cresswell
Animals   Fantasy   Humour

8-11

Henrietta Branford
Philippa Gregory
Mary Hoffman
Penelope Lively

Margaret Ryan
Angie Sage
Pat Thomson

Dragon Ride
The Little Sea Horse
The Sea Piper

Gillian Cross
Adventure   Friends   School

8-11 12-14

Michael Coleman
Dyan Sheldon
Alexander McCall Smith

Pat Thomson
Bob Wilson
David Henry Wilson

The Monster from Underground
Posh Watson

John Cunliffe
Friends   Humour

Allan Ahlberg
Vivian French
Sally Grindley

Margaret Nash
Jillian Powell

Postman Pat Makes a Present
Postman Pat Plant Sitter
Postman Pat's Holiday Packing

Chris d'Lacey
Animals   Family   Humour

8-11 12-14

Allan Ahlberg
Tony Bradman
Pippa Goodhart
Bel Mooney

Michael Morpurgo
Alison Ritchie
Selina Young

Dexter's Journey
Henry Spaloosh!
Juggling with Jeremy
Lofty

Roald Dahl

Fantasy   Humour

8-11

Laurence Anholt
Adrian Boote
Tony Bradman
Herbie Brennan
Keith Brumpton

June Crebbin
Sam McBratney
Francesca Simon
Jeremy Strong
Bob Wilson

Fantastic Mr Fox
The Magic Finger
The Twits

Jenny Dale

Animals

8-11

Phyllis Arkle
Peter Clover
Lucy Daniels
Adèle Geras
Rose Impey

Dick King-Smith
Tessa Krailing
K M Peyton
Alison Prince
Jill Tomlinson

Kitten Tales Series
Pony Tales Series
Puppy Tales Series

Lucy Daniels

Animals   Friends

8-11

Peter Clover
Jenny Dale
Jane Gardam
Elizabeth Hawkins

Dick King-Smith
Tessa Krailing
K M Peyton

Animal Ark Pets Series

Don't forget: Picture Books ∗ Genres ∗ Series ∗ Book Prizes ∗ Bibliography ☞

Penny Dolan Animals   Ghost/supernatural   Humour

5-7

Anne Cassidy
Judy Hindley
Anthony Masters
Maggie Moore
Margaret Nash

Jillian Powell
Alison Ritchie
Hilary Robinson
Barry Wade

Eight Enormous Elephants
Flora McQuack
Mary and the Fairy
Plip and Plop

Julia Donaldson   Animals   Fantasy

Joyce Dunbar
Jan Fearnley

Michael Morpurgo
Hiawyn Oram

The Dinosaur's Diary
Follow the Swallow
The Gruffalo
Monkey Puzzle

Andrew Donkin   Adventure   Ghost/supernatural   Humour

Eleanor Allen
Sarah Garland
Sam Godwin
Sam McBratney

Anthony Masters
Barbara Mitchelhill
Michael Rosen
Theresa Tomlinson

Colour Me Crazy
Cosmic Kev
Night Skies
The Unsinkable Titanic

Malachy Doyle   Historical   Humour   Mythology

12-14

Dennis Hamley
Geraldine McCaughrean

Kirsty White

The Children of Nuala
The Great Hunger
Little People, Big People
12,000 Miles From Home

15

Joyce Dunbar   Animals   Friends

Julia Donaldson
Jan Fearnley
Vivian French
Arnold Lobel

James Marshall
Michael Morpurgo
Jan Page

Gander's Pond
Magic Lemonade
Panda's New Toy
The Ups and Downs of Mouse and Mole

Helen Dunmore   Family   Friends

8-11 12-14

Rachel Anderson
Claire Bevan
Anne Fine

Jamila Gavin
Jan Mark
Bel Mooney

Allie Away
Allie's Rabbit
Amina's Blanket

Alan Durant   Ghost/supernatural   Humour   Sport

8-11 12-14

Janet Burchett and
    Sarah Vogler
Rob Childs
Michael Coleman

June Crebbin
Douglas Hill
Paul Stewart

Kicking Off
Spider McDrew
Creepe Hall Series

P D Eastman   Humour

Allan Ahlberg
Stan and Jan Berenstain
Bennett Cerf

Theo Le Sieg
Dr Seuss

Are You My Mother?
Go Dog Go
Sam and the Firefly

Dorothy Edwards

5-7

Family   Friends   Humour

Joyce Lancaster Brisley
Ann Cameron
Jamila Gavin
Mary Hoffman

Bel Mooney
Magdalen Nabb
Alf Prøysen
Jean Ure

My Naughty Little Sister
My Naughty Little Sister and Bad Harry
More My Naughty Little Sister Stories

Jonathan Emmett

Adventure   Humour   Magic

Jonathan Allen
Roy Apps
Adrian Boote

Philippa Gregory
Ann Jungman
Jill Murphy

Ghostly Goulash
Goblin Stew
Serpent Soup

Jan Fearnley

Humour

June Crebbin
Julia Donaldson

Joyce Dunbar
Frank Rodgers

Colin and the Curly Claw
Mabel and Max

Anne Fine

Family   Fantasy   Friends   Ghost/supernatural

8-11 12-14

Theresa Breslin
June Crebbin
Helen Dunmore
Jane Gardam
Adèle Geras

Robert Leeson
Jan Mark
Michael Morpurgo
Ann Pilling
Jacqueline Wilson

Care of Henry
Countdown
The Haunting of Pip Parker
Roll Over Roly
Stranger Danger

Vivian French

5-7

Animals Humour

Allan Ahlberg
Damon Burnard
John Cunliffe
Joyce Dunbar
Sally Grindley

Arnold Lobel
Shoo Rayner
Pat Thomson
Colin West
Selina Young

Guinea Pigs on the Go
Iggy Pig Series
Space Dog Series

Jane Gardam

Animals Environment Family

Judy Allen
Peter Clover
Lucy Daniels

Anne Fine
Jan Mark

The Kit Stories
Tufty Bear

Sarah Garland

Adventure Family Ghost/supernatural Humour

Eleanor Allen
Judy Allen
Jon Blake

Theresa Breslin
Andrew Donkin
Sam McBratney

Clive and the Missing Finger
Dad on the Run
Madame Sizzers

Susan Gates

Adventure Fantasy Humour School

8-11 12-14

Jeff Brown
Douglas Hill
Ann Jungman

Tessa Krailing
Penelope Lively
Margaret Nash

Beware the Killer Coat
Bill's Baggy Trousers
Return of the Killer Coat

Jamila Gavin
Family   Friends   Mythology   Other cultures

8-11 12-14

Rachel Anderson
Claire Bevan
Malorie Blackman
Lisa Bruce

Ann Cameron
Helen Dunmore
Dorothy Edwards
Julia Jarman

Deadly Friend
Fine Feathered Friend
Kamla and Kate
Monkey in the Stars

Adèle Geras
Animals   Ballet   Family

8-11 12-14

Brian Ball
Antonia Barber
Harriet Castor
Jenny Dale
Anne Fine

Angela Kanter
Tessa Krailing
Jan Mark
K M Peyton
Alison Prince

Blossom's Revenge
Callie's Kittens
Good Luck Louisa
Louisa on Screen

Sam Godwin
Ghost/supernatural

Eleanor Allen
Andrew Donkin
Anthony Masters

Barbara Mitchelhill
Theresa Tomlinson

The Headmaster's Ghost
Picture of Evil
Welcome to the Waxworks

Pippa Goodhart
Animals   Fantasy

Henrietta Branford
Chris d'Lacey
Mary Hoffman

Sheila Lavelle
Penelope Lively
Michael Morpurgo

Catnapped
Happy Sad
Molly and the Beanstalk
Peter and the Waterwolf

Mick Gowar

Adventure Historical Humour School

Scoular Anderson
Theresa Breslin
Keith Brumpton
Mary Hooper

Andrew Matthews
Catherine Sefton
Karen Wallace

The Day We Brightened Up the School
The Guard Dog Geese
The Lost Legionary

Philippa Gregory

Adventure Magic

Roy Apps
Henrietta Branford
Helen Cresswell

Jonathan Emmett
Ann Jungman
Alf Prøysen

Florizella and the Giant
Florizella and the Wolves

Sally Grindley

Adventure Animals

John Cunliffe
Vivian French
Judy Hindley
Alan MacDonald
James Marshall

Kara May
Barbara Mitchelhill
Nicola Moon
Chris Powling
Margaret Ryan

The Giant Postman
Mulberry Goes to School
Mulberry Home Alone

Dennis Hamley

Historical War 1939-45

8-11 12-14

Roy Apps
Jon Blake
Malachy Doyle

Robert Swindells
Karen Wallace
Kirsty White

D Day
Flying Bombs
Tunnel Rescue

Elizabeth Hawkins

Phyllis Arkle
Henrietta Branford
Peter Clover

Lucy Daniels
Tessa Krailing
Hiawyn Oram

Hamster in Danger
A Monster of a Hamster

Douglas Hill

Adventure   Fantasy   Science fiction

8-11

Malorie Blackman
Jeff Brown
Keith Brumpton
Alan Durant

Susan Gates
Julia Jarman
Paul Stewart
Jean Ure

The Magical Tree-Castle
Space Girls Don't Cry

Judy Hindley

Animals   Family   Humour

Alan Baron
Penny Dolan
Sally Grindley

Anita Jeram
Chris Powling
Phyllis Root

The Best Thing About a Puppy
The Perfect Little Monster
Princess Rosa's Winter

Mary Hoffman

Adventure   Animals   Fantasy   Humour

Lisa Bruce
Helen Cresswell
Dorothy Edwards
Pippa Goodhart

Sheila Lavelle
Geraldine McCaughrean
Catherine Sefton

Comet
Dracula's Daughter

Don't forget: Picture Books * Genres * Series * Book Prizes * Bibliography ☞

21

Mary Hooper

Adventure   Family   Historical   Humour

8-11 12-14

Judy Allen
Simon Cheshire
Michael Coleman
Mick Gowar
Julia Jarman

Hilary McKay
Margaret Nash
Karen Wallace
Jacqueline Wilson

The Great Twin Trick
Poppy's Secret
Spooks Ahoy
Spook Summer

Rose Impey

Animals   Family   Humour   Traditional

8-11

Laurence Anholt
Brian Ball
Alan Baron
Jenny Dale
Robert Leeson

Andrew Matthews
Tony Mitton
Maggie Moore
Michael Morpurgo
Hiawyn Oram

Animal Crackers Series
Twice Upon a Time Series

Julia Jarman

Adventure   Family   Humour   Magic

8-11

Scoular Anderson
Roy Apps
Malorie Blackman
Ann Cameron
Jamila Gavin

Douglas Hill
Mary Hooper
Chris Powling
Pat Thomson
Kaye Umansky

Flying Friends
The Jessame Stories
The Magic Backpack

Anita Jeram

Animals   Humour

Allan Ahlberg
Alan Baron
Stan and Jan Berenstain
Judy Hindley

Jillian Powell
Phyllis Root
Colin West

Birthday Happy, Contrary Mary
Daisy Dare

Ann Jungman

5-7

Adventure   Fantasy   Humour   Magic

8-11

Jonathan Allen
Roy Apps
Terence Blacker
Jonathan Emmett

Susan Gates
Philippa Gregory
Jill Murphy
Margaret Ryan

Broomstick Removals
Broomstick Rescue
Dragon Disasters
Frank N Stein and the Monster in Love
School for Dragons

Angela Kanter

Ballet   Family

Antonia Barber
Adèle Geras

Jean Ure

My Ballerina Sister
My Ballerina Sister on Stage

Dick King-Smith

Animals   Family   Fantasy   Humour

8-11

Judy Allen
Peter Clover
Jenny Dale
Lucy Daniels
Andrew and Paula Martyr

Bel Mooney
Michael Morpurgo
Magdalen Nabb
K M Peyton
Ian Whybrow

Dinosaur School
The Finger Eater
The Guard Dog
The Great Sloth Race
The Magic Carpet Slippers
The Sophie Stories

Jenny Koralek

Family

Wendy Smith
Kaye Umansky

Jacqueline Wilson

Dad, Me and the Dinosaurs
Keeping Secrets

Tessa Krailing   Animals   Friends

8-11

Phyllis Arkle
Tony Bradman
Jenny Dale
Lucy Daniels

Susan Gates
Adèle Geras
Elizabeth Hawkins

The Christmas Kitten
Donkey Rescue
Pony Trouble

Sheila Lavelle   Friends   Humour   Magic   School

8-11

Elizabeth Arnold
Pippa Goodhart
Mary Hoffman
Catherine Sefton

Emily Smith
Kaye Umansky
Bob Wilson

The Big Stink
The Dog Napper
Tiger
Pet Pals Series

Theo Le Sieg   Humour

Allan Ahlberg
Stan and Jan Berenstain
Bennett Cerf

P D Eastman
Dr Seuss

I Wish That I Had Duck Feet
Please Try to Remember the First of Octemper
Wacky Wednesday

Robert Leeson   Adventure   Fantasy   Humour   School

8-11 12-14

Laurence Anholt
Herbie Brennan
Anne Fine
Rose Impey
Andrew Matthews

Tony Mitton
Margaret Nash
Robert Swindells
Jean Ure

The Amazing Adventure of Idle Jack
Never Kiss Frogs!
Smart Girls Forever
Why is the Cow on the Roof?

Joan Lingard

5-7

Theresa Breslin   Jenny Nimmo
Jan Mark

Egg Thieves
River Eyes
Tom and the Tree House

Penelope Lively

Family   Fantasy   Humour

8-11 12-14

Rachel Anderson   Helen Cresswell
Harriet Castor   Susan Gates
June Crebbin   Pippa Goodhart

Debbie and the Little Devil
Dragon Trouble

Arnold Lobel

Animals   Humour

Joyce Dunbar   Nicola Moon
Vivian French   Beatrix Potter
James Marshall   Selina Young

Days with Frog and Toad
Mouse Tales
Owl at Home

Sam McBratney

Adventure   Humour   School   Science fiction

Jon Blake   Andrew Donkin
Jeff Brown   Sarah Garland
Keith Brumpton   Colin McNaughton
Simon Cheshire   Dyan Sheldon
Roald Dahl   Pat Thomson

Art, You're Magic!
Kristel Dimond, Timecop
Oliver Sundew, Tooth Fairy
Stranger From Somewhere in Time

Geraldine McCaughrean   Animals   Humour   Mythology

8-11 12-14

Lisa Bruce
Pomme Clayton
Michael Coleman
Malachy Doyle
Mary Hoffman

Margaret Mahy
Kara May
Margaret Mayo
Hiawyn Oram

Noah and Nelly
Phaeton and the Sun Chariot
Wizziwig and the Sweet Machine
Zeus Conquers the Titans

Alan MacDonald   Family   Friends   Humour   Sport

Harriet Castor
Sally Grindley

Kara May
Alison Ritchie

Leon's Fancy Dress Day
Leon Gets a Scarecut
The Goalie from Nowhere

Hilary McKay   Family   Friends

8-11 12-14

Elizabeth Arnold
Theresa Breslin
Mary Hooper

Ann Pilling
Jacqueline Wilson

Beetle and the Bear
Beetle and the Hamster
Keeping Cotton Tail
The Surprise Party

Marilyn McLaughlin   Adventure   Friends   Humour

Tony Bradman
Kara May
Magdalen Nabb

Jenny Oldfield
Dyan Sheldon
Francesca Simon

Fierce Milly
Fierce Milly and the Amazing Dog
Fierce Milly and the Swizzled Eyes

Colin McNaughton

5-7

Adventure   Humour

Allan Ahlberg
Jon Blake
Sam McBratney

Andrew Matthews
Dr Seuss

Captain Abdul's Pirate School
Jolly Roger and the Pirates of Abdul the Skinhead

Margaret Mahy

Humour   Mythology

8-11 12-14

Pomme Clayton
Geraldine McCaughrean

Margaret Mayo
Tony Mitton

Burning the Books
The Great Piratical Rumbustification
Hermes Tricks the Gods
The Wooden Horse

Jan Mark

Family   Friends   Humour   School

8-11 12-14

Rachel Anderson
Claire Bevan
Theresa Breslin
Helen Dunmore
Anne Fine

Jane Gardam
Adèle Geras
Joan Lingard
Jacqueline Wilson

Lady Long-Legs
The Snow Maze
Taking the Cat's Way Home

James Marshall

Animals   Humour

Marc Brown
Joyce Dunbar
Sally Grindley

Arnold Lobel
Shoo Rayner

Fox at Work
Fox on Stage
Fox Outfoxed

Don't forget: Picture Books * Genres * Series * Book Prizes * Bibliography ☞

Andrew and Paula Martyr   Animals   Humour

Brian Ball
Dick King-Smith
Hilda Offen

Daniel Postgate
Frank Rodgers
Pat Thomson

Dog Blaster
Space Dog Shock

Anthony Masters   Animals   Ghost/supernatural   Humour

8-11 12-14

Eleanor Allen
Penny Dolan
Andrew Donkin
Sam Godwin

Barbara Mitchelhill
Nicola Moon
Theresa Tomlinson

Beware the Wicked Web
Deadly Dodgem
Ricky's Rat Gang

Andrew Matthews   Adventure   Historical   Magic   Traditional

8-11

Laurence Anholt
Humphrey Carpenter
Mick Gowar
Rose Impey

Robert Leeson
Colin McNaughton
Maggie Moore

The Emperor's New Clothes
Family Stuff
Galactacus the Awesome
The Little Mermaid
The Runaway Slave

Kara May   Adventure   Animals   Humour   Magic

Brian Ball
Sally Grindley
Geraldine McCaughrean
Alan MacDonald
Marilyn McLaughlin

Nicola Moon
Hilda Offen
Daniel Postgate
Dyan Sheldon
Karen Wallace

Joe Lion's Big Boots
Monkey Business
Emily H Series

Margaret Mayo — Mythology

Pomme Clayton
Geraldine McCaughrean

Margaret Mahy

How Men and Women Were Made
How the Earth Was Made
Why the Sea is Salt

Barbara Mitchelhill — Family   Ghost/supernatural   Humour

Eleanor Allen
Andrew Donkin
Sam Godwin

Sally Grindley
Anthony Masters
Theresa Tomlinson

Eric and the Green-Eyed God
Eric and the Wishing Stone
The Root of Evil
Terror in the Attic

Tony Mitton — Humour   Mythology

Laurence Anholt
Rose Impey
Robert Leeson

Margaret Mahy
Michael Rosen

Great Greek Myth Raps
Robin Hood Raps
Scary Raps

Nicola Moon — Animals   Family   Humour

Sally Grindley
Arnold Lobel
Anthony Masters

Kara May
Jillian Powell

Alligator Tails and Crocodile Cakes
J J Rabbit and the Monster

Don't forget: Picture Books * Genres * Series * Book Prizes * Bibliography ☞

29

Bel Mooney
Family　Humour

12-14

Joyce Lancaster Brisley
Chris d'Lacey
Helen Dunmore
Dorothy Edwards
Dick King-Smith

Magdalen Nabb
Jenny Oldfield
Alison Ritchie
Francesca Simon
Jean Ure

I Don't Want to Say Yes!
It's Not My Fault!
Kitty and Friends Series

Maggie Moore
Humour　Traditional

Anne Cassidy
Penny Dolan
Rose Impey

Andrew Matthews
Barry Wade

Jack and the Beanstalk
Little Red Riding Hood
The Three Little Pigs

Michaela Morgan
Adventure　Animals　Humour

Chris Powling
Margaret Ryan

Dee Shulman

Sausage and the Spooks
Sausage in Trouble
Sick as a Parrot

Michael Morpurgo
Animals　Family　Historical

8-11 12-14

Chris d'Lacey
Julia Donaldson
Joyce Dunbar
Anne Fine
Pippa Goodhart

Rose Impey
Dick King-Smith
Hiawyn Oram
Jill Paton Walsh

Black Queen
The Butterfly Lion
Mairi's Mermaid
Mossop's Last Chance

Jill Murphy — Humour Magic

8-11

Jonathan Allen
Terence Blacker
Humphrey Carpenter

Jonathan Emmett
Ann Jungman

The Worst Witch
The Worst Witch All at Sea
The Worst Witch Strikes Again

Magdalen Nabb — Family Friends

8-11

Dorothy Edwards
Dick King-Smith
Marilyn McLaughlin

Bel Mooney
Jenny Oldfield
Jean Ure

Josie Smith at the Seaside
Josie Smith in Hospital
Josie Smith in Spring

Margaret Nash — Animals Historical Humour School

Tony Bradman
Anne Cassidy
John Cunliffe
Penny Dolan
Susan Gates

Mary Hooper
Robert Leeson
Jillian Powell
Alison Ritchie
Hilary Robinson

The Best Snowman
The Bossy Cockerel
Annie: the Story of a Victorian Mill Girl

Jenny Nimmo — Animals Family Fantasy Magic

8-11 12-14

Theresa Breslin
Joan Lingard
Jan Page

Angie Sage
Colin West

Beak and Whisker
Delilah Alone
Delilah and the Dog Spell
Toby in the Dark
Tom and the Pterosaur

Hilda Offen

Adventure Family

Brian Ball
Lisa Bruce
Andrew and Paula Martyr

Kara May
Hiawyn Oram
Daniel Postgate

Arise Our Rita
Rita in Wonderland
Roll Up! Roll Up! It's Rita

Jenny Oldfield

Friends Humour School

8-11

Marilyn McLaughlin
Bel Mooney
Magdalen Nabb

Francesca Simon
Jean Ure

Definitely Daisy Series

Hiawyn Oram

Adventure Animals Humour

Phyllis Arkle
Lisa Bruce
Peter Clover
Julia Donaldson
Elizabeth Hawkins

Rose Impey
Geraldine McCaughrean
Michael Morpurgo
Hilda Offen

Dog to the Rescue
The Fairies Arrive

Mona the Vampire Series

Jan Page

Humour Magic

Scoular Anderson
Joyce Dunbar
Jenny Nimmo

Frank Rodgers
Catherine Sefton
Wendy Smith

The Chocolate Monster
Dog on a Broomstick
It's Not Funny!

Brian Patten Family   Humour

5-7

Judy Allen   Martin Waddell
Jon Blake   Karen Wallace

Impossible Parents
The Impossible Parents Go Green

K M Peyton Pony/horse

8-11 12-14

Phyllis Arkle   Adèle Geras
Peter Clover   Dick King-Smith
Jenny Dale   Jill Tomlinson
Lucy Daniels

The Paradise Pony
The Pony That Went to Sea
The Scruffy Pony

Ann Pilling Family   Humour

8-11

Rachel Anderson   Anne Fine
Elizabeth Arnold   Hilary McKay
Claire Bevan   Jacqueline Wilson

The Baked Bean Kids
Dustbin Charlie
No Guns, No Oranges

Daniel Postgate Adventure   Family   Humour

Brian Ball   Kara May
Andrew and Paula Martyr   Hilda Offen

Cats, Dogs and Crocodiles
Ghost Train
Super Molly and the Lolly Rescue

Don't forget: Picture Books ★ Genres ★ Series ★ Book Prizes ★ Bibliography ☞

Beatrix Potter
Animals   Family

Arnold Lobel
Jill Tomlinson

Alison Uttley

The Tale of Benjamin Bunny
The Tale of Peter Rabbit

Jillian Powell
Animals   Family   Humour

Alan Baron
Anne Cassidy
John Cunliffe
Penny Dolan
Anita Jeram

Nicola Moon
Margaret Nash
Alison Ritchie
Hilary Robinson
Phyllis Root

The Lazy Scarecrow
The Naughty Puppy
Recycled

Chris Powling
Adventure   Family   Humour

Marc Brown
Sally Grindley
Judy Hindley
Julia Jarman
Michaela Morgan

Margaret Ryan
Dyan Sheldon
Pat Thomson
Bob Wilson
Philip Wooderson

A Ghost Behind the Stairs
Kit's Castle
Rover Goes to School

Alison Prince
Animals   Humour

8-11 12-14

Harriet Castor
Jenny Dale

Adèle Geras

Bumble
Cat Number 3
Dog Called You

Alf Prøysen

Adventure   Fantasy   Humour   Magic

Jeff Brown
Dorothy Edwards

Philippa Gregory
Jeremy Strong

Mrs Pepperpot Stories
Mrs Pepperpot Again
Mrs Pepperpot's Year

Shoo Rayner

Adventure   Animals   Humour

Allan Ahlberg
Jonathan Allen
Lindsay Camp
Harriet Castor
Vivian French

James Marshall
Michael Rosen
Angie Sage
Nick Sharratt
Martin Waddell

The Pumpkin Man
Super Dad the Super Hero
Treacle Treacle, Little Tart
Tunnel Mazers

Alison Ritchie

Animals   Family   Humour

Anne Cassidy
Chris d'Lacey
Penny Dolan
Alan MacDonald
Bel Mooney

Margaret Nash
Jillian Powell
Margaret Ryan
Nick Sharratt
Selina Young

Horrible Haircut
Riff-Raff Rabbit

Hilary Robinson

Animals   Humour

Stan and Jan Berenstain
Anne Cassidy
Penny Dolan

Margaret Nash
Jillian Powell
Nick Sharratt

Freddie's Fears
Mr Spotty's Potty

Frank Rodgers

Animals   Humour   Magic

Scoular Anderson
Marc Brown
Jan Fearnley
Andrew and Paula Martyr
Jan Page

Alexander McCall Smith
Wendy Smith
Kaye Umansky
Martin Waddell
Colin West

Mr Croc's Clock
The Robodog and the Big Dig
The Witch's Dog and the Ice Cream Wizard

Phyllis Root

Animals   Humour

Alan Baron
Judy Hindley
Anita Jeram

Jillian Powell
Colin West

Foggy Friday
Meow Monday
Soggy Saturday

Michael Rosen

Humour

Jonathan Allen
Andrew Donkin

Tony Mitton
Shoo Rayner

Clever Cakes and Other Stories
Even Stevens FC
Lunch Boxes Don't Fly
Mission Ziffoid
Uncle Billy Being Silly

Margaret Ryan

Adventure   Family   Humour

Judy Allen
Helen Cresswell
Sally Grindley
Ann Jungman
Michaela Morgan

Chris Powling
Alison Ritchie
Dyan Sheldon
Dee Shulman
Karen Wallace

Captain Motley and the Pirate Gold
The Disappearing Dinner
Harry and the Tiger
The Littlest Dragon at School
Smudger and the Smelly Fish

Angie Sage

Animals   Family   Fantasy   Humour

Judy Allen
Brian Ball
Helen Cresswell

Jenny Nimmo
Shoo Rayner
Martin Waddell

Allie's Crocodile
Crocodile Canal
Mouse
Shark Island

Catherine Sefton

Ghost/supernatural   Humour   Magic

is Martin Wardell   8-11

Eleanor Allen
Harriet Castor
Mick Gowar
Mary Hoffman

Sheila Lavelle
Jan Page
Kaye Umansky
Jill Paton Walsh

The Day the Smells Went Wrong
The Pocket Elephant
Watch Out, Fred's About

Dr Seuss

Humour

Allan Ahlberg
Stan and Jan Berenstain
Marc Brown
Bennett Cerf

P D Eastman
Theo Le Sieg
Colin McNaughton

The Cat in the Hat
Fox in Socks
Green Eggs and Ham

Nick Sharratt

Humour

June Crebbin
Shoo Rayner
Alison Ritchie

Hilary Robinson
Martin Waddell

Caveman Dave
The Green Queen
Monday Run-day

Dyan Sheldon — Adventure   Friends   Humour   School

8-11 12-14

Judy Allen
Jon Blake
Simon Cheshire
Gillian Cross
Sam McBratney

Marilyn McLaughlin
Kara May
Chris Powling
Margaret Ryan
Alexander McCall Smith

Elena the Frog
Harry's Holiday
Lizzie and Charley Go to the Movies

Dee Shulman — Adventure   Ghost/supernatural   Humour

Scoular Anderson
Michaela Morgan

Margaret Ryan

Magenta and the Ghost Babies
Magenta and the Ghost School
Magenta and the Scary Ghosts
My Mum

Francesca Simon — Family   Humour   School

8-11

Marc Brown
Ann Cameron
Simon Cheshire
Roald Dahl
Marilyn McLaughlin

Bel Mooney
Jenny Oldfield
Jeremy Strong
Ian Whybrow
David Henry Wilson

Horrid Henry and the Mummy's Curse
Horrid Henry and the Secret Club
Horrid Henry Tricks the Tooth Fairy

Alexander McCall Smith — Adventure   Friends   Humour

Jon Blake
Jeff Brown
Ann Cameron
Gillian Cross

Frank Rodgers
Dyan Sheldon
Jeremy Strong
David Henry Wilson

Monkey Boy
The Popcorn Pirates

Emily Smith

5-7

Adventure   Family   Friends   Humour

also writes as E F Smith

Elizabeth Arnold
Ann Cameron
Sheila Lavelle

Jean Ure
Bob Wilson
Jacqueline Wilson

Annie and the Aliens
Astrid the Au Pair from Outer Space
The Shrimp

Wendy Smith

Family   Friends   Humour   Magic

Scoular Anderson
Brian Ball
Jenny Koralek
Jan Page

Frank Rodgers
Kaye Umansky
Jacqueline Wilson

Billy the Conkerer
Bubblegum Brother
Crazy Magic
Magic Hotel

Paul Stewart

Family   Humour   Science fiction

8-11

Scoular Anderson
Damon Burnard
Alan Durant

Douglas Hill
Jeremy Strong

Dogbird
Naughty Gnomes
Purple Alert
The Were-Pig

The Blobheads Series

Jeremy Strong

Adventure   Family   Fantasy   Humour

8-11

Adrian Boote
Jeff Brown
Keith Brumpton
Roald Dahl
Alf Prøysen

Francesca Simon
Alexander McCall Smith
Paul Stewart
David Henry Wilson

Dinosaur Pox
Giant Jim and the Hurricane
Just a Bit of Wind
My Dad's Got an Alligator

5-7

Robert Swindells · Fantasy War 1939-45

8-11 12-14

Dennis Hamley · Robert Leeson

Hurricane Summer
The Ice Palace
Roger's War

Pat Thomson · Animals Family Humour School

Allan Ahlberg
Scoular Anderson
Damon Burnard
Helen Cresswell
Gillian Cross

Vivian French
Julia Jarman
Sam McBratney
Andrew and Paula Martyr
Chris Powling

Rhyming Russell
Talking Pictures

Jill Tomlinson · Animals Humour

Phyllis Arkle
Henrietta Branford
Peter Clover
Jenny Dale

K M Peyton
Beatrix Potter
Alison Uttley

The Cat Who Wanted to Go Home
The Hen Who Wouldn't Give Up
The Owl Who Was Afraid of the Dark

Theresa Tomlinson · Ghost/supernatural

8-11 12-14

Eleanor Allen
Andrew Donkin
Sam Godwin

Anthony Masters
Barbara Mitchelhill
Jill Paton Walsh

Haunted House Blues
Meet Me by the Steelmen
The Night of the Red Devil

Kaye Umansky

Fantasy Humour Magic

8-11

Roy Apps
Humphrey Carpenter
Julia Jarman
Jenny Koralek
Sheila Lavelle

Frank Rodgers
Catherine Sefton
Wendy Smith
Jean Ure

The Dressed-up Giant
The Romantic Giant
The Spooks Step Out
Three Days with Jim

Jean Ure

Adventure Animals Friends School

8-11 12-14

Antonia Barber
Dorothy Edwards
Douglas Hill
Angela Kanter
Robert Leeson

Bel Mooney
Magdalen Nabb
Jenny Oldfield
Emily Smith
Kaye Umansky

Big Head
Bonnie
Danny Dynamite
The Unknown Planet

Sandy Simmons Series

Alison Uttley

Animals

8-11

Beatrix Potter

Jill Tomlinson

Little Grey Rabbit Series
Sam Pig Series

Don't forget: Picture Books * Genres * Series * Book Prizes * Bibliography ☞

Martin Waddell
Adventure Animals Humour Sport

also writes as Catherine Sefton   8-11 12-14

Judy Allen
Keith Brumpton
Janet Burchett and
   Sarah Vogler
Michael Coleman
June Crebbin

Brian Patten
Shoo Rayner
Frank Rodgers
Angie Sage
Nick Sharratt

Cup Final Kid
Millie Bean, Jungle Queen
The Perils of Lord Reggie Parrot
Two Brown Bears

Barry Wade
Humour Traditional

Anne Cassidy
Penny Dolan

Maggie Moore

Cinderella
Goldilocks and the Three Bears
The Three Billy Goats Gruff

Karen Wallace
Adventure Family Historical Humour

8-11

Roy Apps
Lisa Bruce
Michael Coleman
Mick Gowar
Dennis Hamley

Mary Hooper
Kara May
Brian Patten
Margaret Ryan
Philip Wooderson

The Case of the Disappearing Necklace
Drakes Special Delivery
Marvin, the Blue Pig
Tutankhamun's Arrow

Freaky Families Series

Don't forget: Picture Books * Genres * Series * Book Prizes * Bibliography ☞

42

Jill Paton Walsh Fantasy Ghost/supernatural Historical

5-7

12-14

Michael Morpurgo   Theresa Tomlinson
Catherine Sefton

Birdy and the Ghosties
Matthew and the Sea Singer
Thomas and the Tinners

Colin West   Animals Family Humour

Phyllis Arkle   Jenny Nimmo
Alan Baron   Frank Rodgers
Stan and Jan Berenstain   Phyllis Root
Vivian French   Philip Wooderson
Anita Jeram

"I Don't Care!" Said the Bear
Mr Potts the Potty Teacher
Uncle and Aunty Pat

Kirsty White   Historical

Malachy Doyle   Dennis Hamley

Over the Sea to Skye
A Queen's Promise
Stranger in the Glen

Ian Whybrow   Adventure Animals Humour Letters

8-11

Marc Brown   Dick King-Smith
Damon Burnard   Francesca Simon
Simon Cheshire   David Henry Wilson

Aliens Stole My Dog
Harry and the Dinosaurs say "Raahh!"
Holly and the Skyboard
Whizz the Fleabag
Little Wolf Series

Bob Wilson — Friends   Humour   School   Sport

Laurence Anholt
Janet Burchett and
    Sarah Vogler
Rob Childs
Michael Coleman

Gillian Cross
Roald Dahl
Sheila Lavelle
Chris Powling
Emily Smith

Daring Dan
Football Fred
Lucky Lily
Monica's Monster
Rashid's Rescue

David Henry Wilson — Adventure   Family   Humour

Simon Cheshire
Gillian Cross
Francesca Simon

Alexander McCall Smith **8-11**
Jeremy Strong
Ian Whybrow

Do Gerbils Go to Heaven?
How the Lion Lost his Lunch
Never Say Moo to a Bull

Jacqueline Wilson — Adventure   Family   Fantasy   Humour

8-11 12-14

Theresa Breslin
Simon Cheshire
Anne Fine
Mary Hooper
Jenny Koralek

Hilary McKay
Jan Mark
Ann Pilling
Emily Smith
Wendy Smith

Lizzie Zipmouth
The Monster Storyteller
Monster's Eyeballs
My Brother Bernadette

Philip Wooderson

Adventure   Historical   Humour

5-7

Scoular Anderson   Karen Wallace
Chris Powling   Colin West

Arf and the Greedy Grabber
Arf and the Metal Detector
The Scrunchy Scarab

Selina Young

Animals   Friends   Humour

Tony Bradman   Arnold Lobel
Chris d'Lacey   Alison Ritchie
Vivian French

Big Dog and Little Dog Go Sailing
Big Dog and Little Dog Visit the Moon

Don't forget: Picture Books * Genres * Series * Book Prizes * Bibliography ☞

45

Authors for Ages 8-11

8-11

Richard Adams — Animals Environment Fantasy

Colin Dann   Brian Jacques

Plague Dogs
Watership Down

Allan Ahlberg — Family Fantasy Humour School

5-7

Tony Bradman   Hazel Townson
Catherine Storr   David Henry Wilson
Jeremy Strong

The Bear Nobody Wanted
The Better Brown Stories
My Brother's Ghost
Ten in a Bed
Woof!

Joan Aiken — Adventure Family Fantasy Ghost/supernatural

12-14

Henrietta Branford   Garry Kilworth
Kevin Crossley-Holland   William Nicholson
Robin Jarvis   Philip Pullman
Diana Wynne Jones   Celia Rees
Terry Jones   Catherine Storr

Bone and Dream
The Wolves of Willoughby Chase

James III Series
St Boan Mysteries

Vivien Alcock — Family Fantasy Ghost/supernatural

12-14

Annie Dalton   Jenny Nimmo
Diana Hendry

The Boy Who Swallowed a Ghost
Haunting of Cassie Palmer
The Stonewalker

Louisa May Alcott
Family

Frances Hodgson Burnett
Susan M Coolidge
Hilary McKay

L M Montgomery
Johanna Spyri
Laura Ingalls Wilder

Good Wives
Jo's Boys
Little Women

8-11

David Almond
Family   Fantasy

12-14

Lynne Reid Banks
Melvin Burgess
Berlie Doherty
Jostein Gaarder
Clive King

Jan Mark
Andrew Norriss
Stephen Potts
Susan Price

Skellig

Rachel Anderson   Family   Historical   Sci fiction   War 1939-45

5-7 12-14

Julie Bertagna
Michelle Magorian

Michael Morpurgo
Alison Prince

The Flight of the Emu
Joe's Story
Princess Jazz and the Angels
The Scavenger's Tale
Tough as Old Boots
The War Orphan

Laurence Anholt
Humour

5-7

Henrietta Branford
Herbie Brennan
Keith Brumpton
Andrew Davies

Gail Carson Levine
Margaret Mahy
Francesca Simon

Eco-Wolf and the Three Pigs
Little Red Riding Wolf
The One and Only Series
Seriously Silly Stories Series

47

Roy Apps

Adventure Fantasy Historical Humour

5-7

Morris Gleitzman   Jeremy Strong
Paul Jennings   Alan Temperley
Gary Paulsen

Anne Frank: the Last Days of Freedom
Melvin the Avenger
Melvin and the Deadheads
Stacey Stone: a Rat's Tale

Aunt Boomerang Series
How to Handle Series

Philip Ardagh

Humour

Steve Barlow and   Cliff McNish
   Steve Skidmore   Philip Ridley
Morris Gleitzman   Lemony Snicket

Awful End
Dreadful Acts
The Fall of Fergus

Neil Arksey

Sport

12-14

Bernard Ashley   Alan Durant
Terence Blacker   Alan Gibbons
Rob Childs   Michael Hardcastle
Michael Coleman   Paul May
Chris d'Lacey

Brooksie
Flint
Result
Sudden Death

Mary Arrigan

Ghost/supernatural Historical

Alan Garner   Paul Stewart
Jamila Gavin   Catherine Storr
Jenny Nimmo

Baldur's Bones
Ghost Bird
Grimstone's Ghost

8-11

Bernard Ashley

Family   School   Sport

12-14

Neil Arksey
Julie Bertagna
Terence Blacker
Anne Fine
Alan Gibbons

Gene Kemp
Robert Leeson
Jan Mark
Jenny Oldfield
Jean Ure

Dinner Ladies Don't Count
Justin Strikes Again
Who Loves You, Billy?
Your Guess is as Good as Mine

8-11

Enid Bagnold

Animals   Pony/horse

K M Peyton

Anna Sewell

National Velvet

Lynne Reid Banks

Family   Fantasy

12-14

David Almond
Lucy M Boston
Stephen Elboz
Elizabeth Goudge
Clive King

Penelope Lively
E Nesbit
Mary Norton
Sylvia Waugh

Harry the Poisonous Centipede
The Indian in the Cupboard
The Key to the Indian
The Mystery of the Cupboard
Return of the Indian
The Secret of the Indian

Antonia Barber

Ballet   Historical   Stage

5-7

Emily Costello
Adèle Geras

Mal Lewis Jones
Noel Streatfeild

Lucy's Next Step
Model Dancers
The Mousehole Cat
Dancing Shoes Series

Steve Barlow and Steve Skidmore — Humour

Philip Ardagh
Kathryn Cave
Roald Dahl
Terry Deary

Clive Dickinson
Mark Haddon
Russell Stannard

Vernon Bright and the End of the World
Vernon Bright and the Faster-than-Light Show
Vernon Bright and Frankenstein's Hamster
Vernon Bright and the Magnetic Banana

J M Barrie — Fantasy

Frank L Baum
Lewis Carroll
Russell Hoban

C S Lewis
P L Travers
Sylvia Waugh

Peter Pan

Frank L Baum — Fantasy

J M Barrie
Lewis Carroll

C S Lewis
P L Travers

The Wizard of Oz

Nina Bawden — Adventure   Det mysteries   Family   War 1939-45

Theresa Breslin
Andrew Davies
Berlie Doherty
Jackie French
Adèle Geras

Judith Kerr
Michelle Magorian
Linda Newberry
Ann Turnbull

Carrie's War
The Finding
Keeping Henry
The Peppermint Pig
The Secret Passage

Don't forget: Picture Books * Genres * Series * Book Prizes * Bibliography ☞

Julie Bertagna
Animals   Family   Humour   Social issues

12-14

Rachel Anderson   Jan Mark
Bernard Ashley

Bungee Hero
Dolphin Boy
Ice Cream Machine

8-11

Terence Blacker
Adventure   Computers   Humour   Sport

5-7 12-14

Neil Arksey   Alan Durant
Bernard Ashley   Alan Gibbons
Tony Bradman   Michael Hardcastle
Rob Childs   Kate Saunders
Michael Coleman   Martin Waddell

Dream Team
Shooting Star
The Transfer
Ms Wiz series

Malorie Blackman
Adventure   Computers   Det myst   Social iss

5-7 12-14

Theresa Breslin   Alan Gibbons
Michael Coleman   Julia Jarman
Gillian Cross   Helena Pielichaty
Terrance Dicks   Kate Thompson
Jamila Gavin

A.N.T.I.D.O.T.E.
Computer Ghost
Dangerous Reality
Forbidden Game

Thomas Bloor
Detective mysteries   Family

Lemony Snicket   Robert Swindells

Factory of Shadows
The House of Eyes
The Memory Prisoner

8-11

Judy Blume

Family   Humour   School

12-14

Betsy Byars	Robin Klein
Beverly Cleary	Sheila Lavelle
Gillian Cross	Lois Lowry
Paula Danziger	Ruth Symes
Anne Fine	Jacqueline Wilson

Fudge-a-mania
It's Not the End of the World
Otherwise Known as Sheila the Great
Superfudge

Enid Blyton

Adventure   Detective mysteries   School

Elinor M Brent-Dyer	Anthony Masters
Franklin W Dixon	Arthur Ransome
Carolyn Keene	

Famous Five Series
Malory Towers Series
Secret Seven Series

Michael Bond

Animals   Family

Dick King-Smith	A A Milne

Paddington Bear Series

Lucy M Boston

Adventure   Family   Fantasy

Lynne Reid Banks	E Nesbit
Frances Hodgson Burnett	Philippa Pearce
Edward Eager	P L Travers
Penelope Farmer	Alison Uttley
Elizabeth Goudge	Sylvia Waugh

The Children of Green Knowe
The Chimneys of Green Knowe
The River at Green Knowe

*Don't forget: Picture Books * Genres * Series * Book Prizes * Bibliography* ☞

Tony Bradman

Adventure   Environment   School   Sport

5-7

Allan Ahlberg
Terence Blacker
Henrietta Branford
Kathryn Cave
Rob Childs

Terrance Dicks
Susan Gates
Michael Hardcastle
Gail Carson Levine
Jeremy Strong

Aftershock
Hurricane
The Two Jacks
One Nil

8-11

Henrietta Branford

Adventure   Humour

5-7 12-14

Joan Aiken
Laurence Anholt
Tony Bradman
Debi Gliori

Pat Hutchins
Jeremy Strong
Theresa Tomlinson

Dimanche Diller
Dimanche Diller in Danger
Dipper's Island
Spacebaby
Spacebaby and the Megavolt Monster

Herbie Brennan

Adventure   Humour   Letters

5-7

Laurence Anholt
Roald Dahl

Anthony Horowitz

Fairy Nuff: a Tale of Bluebell Wood
Fairy Nuff: Another Tale of Bluebell Wood
Letters from a Mouse

Elinor M Brent-Dyer

School

Enid Blyton
Susan M Coolidge

Adèle Geras

The Chalet School Series

53

Theresa Breslin

Fantasy   Historical   Humour

5-7 12-14

Nina Bawden
Malorie Blackman
Berlie Doherty
Diana Wynne Jones

Enid Richemont
J K Rowling
Alan Temperley

Across the Roman Wall
The Dream Master
Dream Master Nightmare!
Name Games

Keith Brumpton

Fantasy   Humour

5-7

Laurence Anholt
Terry Deary
Susan Gates

Alan Temperley
Martin Waddell
David Henry Wilson

The Green Knight
Kidnapped by Ice Maidens
The Mystery of the Dachshund Diamonds
Nice Throne, Shame About the Crown

Anthony Buckeridge

Humour   School

Richmal Crompton
Gillian Cross

Jean Ure

Jennings as Usual
Jennings Goes to School

Melvin Burgess

Fantasy   Ghost/supernatural   Social issues

12-14

David Almond
Leon Garfield
Ted Hughes

Jenny Nimmo
Gary Paulsen
Paul Stewart

An Angel for May
The Baby and Fly Pie
The Earth Giant
The Ghost Behind the Wall

8-11

Frances Hodgson Burnett Family Historical: Victorian

Louisa May Alcott
Lucy M Boston
Susan M Coolidge
Penelope Farmer

Elizabeth Goudge
E Nesbit
Alison Uttley

Little Lord Fauntleroy
A Little Princess
The Secret Garden

Betsy Byars Computers Family Humour

Judy Blume
Paula Danziger
Robin Klein

Lois Lowry
Ruth Symes

The Computer Nut
The Eighteenth Emergency
The Midnight Fox
The Pinballs

Lewis Carroll Fantasy

J M Barrie
Frank L Baum
Jostein Gaarder
Russell Hoban

C S Lewis
Geraldine McCaughrean
P L Travers

Alice's Adventures in Wonderland
Alice Through the Looking Glass

Kathryn Cave Animals Fantasy Humour

Steve Barlow and
　　Steve Skidmore

Tony Bradman
Jill Murphy

Dragonrise
The Emperor's Gruckle Hound
Henry Hobbs, Space Voyager
Jumble
Septimus Similion, Practising Wizard

Simon Cheshire
Humour   Science fiction

5-7

Mark Haddon
Jeremy Strong

Ian Whybrow
David Henry Wilson

They Melted His Brain
Totally Unsuitable for Children
Jeremy Brown Series

Rob Childs
Sport

5-7

Neil Arksey
Terence Blacker
Tony Bradman
Michael Coleman
Alan Durant

Alan Gibbons
Michael Hardcastle
Paul May
Martin Waddell

Phantom Football
Soccer Showdowns
Time Ranger Series

John Christopher
Ghost/supernatural   Science fiction

Nicholas Fisk
Douglas Hill

Maggie Prince

Empty World
The Prince in Waiting Trilogy
Tripods Trilogy

Beverly Cleary
Family   School

Judy Blume
Helen Cresswell
Mary Hooper

Sheila Lavelle
Frances Thomas
Jacqueline Wilson

The Ramona Series

*Don't forget: Picture Books * Genres * Series * Book Prizes * Bibliography* ☞

David Clement-Davies

Animals   Fantasy

W J Corbett
Colin Dann

Brian Jacques
Garry Kilworth

Fire Bringer
The Sight

Michael Coleman

Adventure   Computers   Sport

5-7

Neil Arksey
Terence Blacker
Malorie Blackman
Rob Childs
Bruce Coville

Chris d'Lacey
Terrance Dicks
Alan Durant
Alan Gibbons
Paul May

The Snog Log
Tag
Triv in Pursuit
Weirdo's War

Internet Detectives Series

Eoin Colfer

Fantasy

12-14

Roald Dahl
Catherine Fisher
Debi Gliori

Michael Hoeye
Terry Pratchett
Philip Ridley

Artemis Fowl
Artemis Fowl: the Arctic Incident
The Wish List

Susan M Coolidge

Family

Louisa May Alcott
Elinor M Brent-Dyer
Frances Hodgson Burnett

L M Montgomery
Johanna Spyri
Laura Ingalls Wilder

What Katy Did
What Katy Did at School
What Katy Did Next

8-11

Susan Cooper

12-14

Annie Dalton
Catherine Fisher
Alan Garner
Robin Jarvis
Geraldine McCaughrean

William Nicholson
Jenny Nimmo
Philip Pullman
J R R Tolkien
T H White

The Boggart
The Boggart and the Monster
Green Boy
The Dark is Rising Series

W J Corbett

David Clement-Davies
Colin Dann
Kenneth Grahame

Brian Jacques
Garry Kilworth

The Battle of Chinnbrook Wood
The Dragon's Egg and Other Stories
Pentecost Trilogy

Emily Costello

Antonia Barber
Jenny Dale
Lucy Daniels

Narinder Dhami
Jenny Oldfield

Abandoned Puppy
Lonely Lamb
Otter Alert

Bruce Coville

Michael Coleman
Mark Haddon

Douglas Hill
Paul Jennings

Farewell to Earth
My Teacher Glows in the Dark
There's an Alien in My Underwear

Sharon Creech
Diaries Family Ghost/supernatural Humour

12-14

Kate di Camillo
Berlie Doherty
Robin Klein

Jan Mark
Katherine Paterson
E F Smith

The Ghost of Uncle Arvie
Love That Dog
Ruby Holler

Helen Cresswell
Adventure Family Fantasy Humour

5-7

Beverly Cleary
Penelope Farmer
Diana Hendry
Diana Wynne Jones

Gail Carson Levine
Penelope Lively
Philippa Pearce
Catherine Storr

Moondial
Posy Bates and the Bag Lady
The Bagthorpe Saga

Richmal Crompton
Family Humour School

Anthony Buckeridge

Paul Jennings

Just William
Sweet William
William at War

Gillian Cross
Adventure Computers Humour School

5-7 12-14

Malorie Blackman
Judy Blume
Anthony Buckeridge
Anthony Horowitz
Gene Kemp

Elizabeth Laird
Hilary McKay
Jan Mark
Arthur Ransome
Jacqueline Wilson

The Great Elephant Chase
The Iron Way
The Monster from the Underground
New World
Wolf

The Demon Headmaster Series

8-11

8-11

Kevin Crossley-Holland — Family Hist: Medieval Mythology Trad

12-14

Joan Aiken
Alan Garner
Grace Hallworth
Cynthia Harnett
Terry Jones

Robert Leeson
Geraldine McCaughrean
Michael Morpurgo
Rosemary Sutcliff
T H White

Arthur: at the Crossing-places
Arthur: the Seeing Stone
The Nightingale that Shrieked
Short!
Why the Fish Laughed

Karen Cushman — Historical: Medieval

12-14

Cynthia Harnett

Rosemary Sutcliff

Catherine, Called Birdy
Matilda Bone
The Midwife's Apprentice

Chris d'Lacey — Adventure Family Social issues Sport

5-7 12-14

Neil Arksey
Michael Coleman
Alan Durant

Michael Morpurgo
Gary Paulsen

The Fire Within
Fly Cherokee, Fly
Pawnee Warrior
The Salt Pirates of Skegness

*Don't forget: Picture Books * Genres * Series * Book Prizes * Bibliography* ☞

Roald Dahl

Fantasy   Humour

5-7

8-11

Steve Barlow and
   Steve Skidmore
Herbie Brennan
Eoin Colfer
Debi Gliori
Diana Hendry

Anthony Horowitz
Eva Ibbotson
Philip Ridley
Lemony Snicket
Ian Whybrow

The BFG
Charlie and the Chocolate Factory
Danny the Champion of the World
James and the Giant Peach
Matilda

Jenny Dale

Animals

5-7

Emily Costello
Lucy Daniels
Narinder Dhami

Rose Impey
Jenny Oldfield

Little Star
Milly's Triumph
Perfect Puppy

Annie Dalton

Family   Fantasy

12-14

Vivien Alcock
Susan Cooper
Catherine Fisher
Pauline Fisk

Diana Hendry
William Nicholson
Susan Price
J K Rowling

Calling the Shots
Friday Forever
Losing the Plot
Paradise High

Afterdark Series

Lucy Daniels

Animals   Diaries

5-7

Emily Costello
Jenny Dale
Wendy Douthwaite
Mary Ellis
Brenda Jobling

Dick King-Smith
Tessa Krailing
Elizabeth Laird
Jenny Oldfield
Anna Sewell

Animal Ark Series
Dolphin Diaries Series

8-11

Colin Dann

Adventure   Animals

Richard Adams
David Clement-Davies
W J Corbett
Kenneth Grahame
Brian Jacques

Dick King-Smith
Elizabeth Laird
Jenny Oldfield
Dodie Smith

Animals of Farthing Wood
Journey to Freedom
Lion Country

Paula Danziger

Family   Humour

12-14

Judy Blume
Betsy Byars
Anne Fine
Mary Hooper

Lois Lowry
Helena Pielichaty
Dyan Sheldon
Francesca Simon

The Cat Ate My Gymsuit
It's Justin Time
Not for a Million Gazillion Dollars

A is for Amber Series

Andrew Davies

Humour   War 1939-45

Laurence Anholt
Nina Bawden

Anne Holm

Conrad's War
Educating Marmalade
Marmalade Hits the Big Time

Hunter Davies Humour

Willis Hall   Hilary McKay
Sheila Lavelle

Flossie Teacake Again
Flossie Teacake's Fur Coat
Flossie Teacake Wins the Lottery
The Snotty Bumstead Collection

8-11

Terry Deary   Historical   Humour

Steve Barlow and   Clive Dickinson
   Steve Skidmore   Ann Jungman
Keith Brumpton   Robert Leeson

Pit Street Pirates
The Prince of Rags and Patches
The Treasure of Crazy Horse

Horrible Histories Series

Narinder Dhami   Animals   Sport

12-14

Emily Costello   Rose Impey
Jenny Dale

Bend It Like Beckham
Caspar in the Spotlight
Me and My Big Mouth
The Sleepover Club Sleep Out
Sleepover Girls Go Karting

Kate di Camillo   Animals   Family   Other lands

Sharon Creech   Katherine Paterson

Because of Winn-Dixie
The Tiger Rising

Don't forget: Picture Books ∗ Genres ∗ Series ∗ Book Prizes ∗ Bibliography ☞

Clive Dickinson

8-11

Diaries   Historical   Humour

Steve Barlow and
    Steve Skidmore
Terry Deary

Anthony Horowitz
Harry Horse

The Lost Diary of Annie Oakley's Wild West Stagehand
The Lost Diary of Christopher Columbus' Look Out
The Lost Diary of Montezuma's Soothsayer

Terrance Dicks

Computers   Science fiction

Malorie Blackman
Tony Bradman
Michael Coleman

Nicholas Fisk
Douglas Hill

The Chinese Ghost Incident
The Nazi Dagger Incident
Virtual Unreality

Franklin W Dixon

Adventure   Detective mysteries

Enid Blyton
Carolyn Keene

Fiona Kelly
Ann M Martin

The Hardy Boys Series

Berlie Doherty

Adventure   Family   Fantasy   Historical

12-14

David Almond
Nina Bawden
Theresa Breslin
Sharon Creech
Anne Fine

Penelope Lively
Geraldine McCaughrean
Linda Newberry
Katherine Paterson
Philippa Pearce

Daughter of the Sea
Granny Was a Buffer Girl
The Sailing Ship Tree

Wendy Douthwaite Animals Pony/horse

Lucy Daniels   K M Peyton
Jenny Oldfield

Dream Pony
The Lost Pony
The Orange Pony
Polly on Location

8-11

Helen Dunmore Adventure Computers School Thrillers

5-7 12-14

Anne Fine   Hilary McKay
Lesley Howarth

Fatal Error
Zillah and Me
The Zillah Rebellion

Alan Durant Humour Sport

5-7 12-14

Neil Arksey   Michael Coleman
Terence Blacker   Chris d'Lacey
Rob Childs   Michael Hardcastle

Barmy Army
K O Kings
Creepe Hall Series
Leggs United Series

Edward Eager Fantasy Magic

Lucy M Boston   E Nesbit
Jill Murphy   Kaye Umansky

Half Magic
Knight's Castle
Magic by the Lake
The Time Garden

Don't forget: Picture Books * Genres * Series * Book Prizes * Bibliography ☞

Stephen Elboz

8-11

Lynne Reid Banks
Diana Hendry
Diana Wynne Jones

Cliff McNish
J K Rowling

Bottle Boy
Ghostlands
A Handful of Magic
House of Rats
A Land Without Magic
The Tower at Moonville

Mary Ellis

Lucy Daniels
Jamila Gavin

Grace Hallworth

The Arctic Fox
Elephant Child
Lily Dragon

Penelope Farmer

Lucy M Boston
Frances Hodgson Burnett
Helen Cresswell
Pauline Fisk
Penelope Lively

Anne Merrick
Magdalen Nabb
Philippa Pearce
Catherine Storr
Alison Uttley

Castle of Bone
Charlotte Sometimes
The Summer Birds
Thicker Than Water

*Don't forget: Picture Books * Genres * Series * Book Prizes * Bibliography* ☞

Anne Fine

Diaries   Family   Humour   School

5-7 12-14

8-11

Bernard Ashley
Judy Blume
Paula Danziger
Berlie Doherty
Helen Dunmore

Gene Kemp
Hilary McKay
Helena Pielichaty
Hazel Townson
Jacqueline Wilson

Bad Dreams
Bill's New Frock
Charm School
Goggle Eyes
Jennifer's Diary
Notso Hotso

Catherine Fisher

Fantasy   Thrillers

12-14

Eoin Colfer
Susan Cooper
Annie Dalton
Alan Garner
Robin Jarvis

Diana Wynne Jones
Garry Kilworth
Jenny Nimmo
Philip Pullman
J K Rowling

Belin's Hill
Book of the Crow Series
The Snow Walker Series

Nicholas Fisk

Fantasy   Horror   Science fiction

John Christopher
Terrance Dicks
Douglas Hill

Maggie Prince
Russell Stannard
R L Stine

Grinny
Monster Maker
A Rag, a Bone and a Hank of Hair

Pauline Fisk

8-11

Adventure Fantasy

Annie Dalton
Penelope Farmer
Diana Wynne Jones

Anne Merrick
Catherine Storr

The Candle House
Midnight Blue
Sabrina Fludde
Telling the Sea
The Tyger Pool

Jackie French

War 1939-45

Nina Bawden
Anne Holm
Judith Kerr
Michelle Magorian

Ian Serraillier
Ann Turnbull
Robert Westall

Hitler's Daughter

Jostein Gaarder

Family   Fantasy   Ghost/supernatural   Magic

12-14

David Almond
Lewis Carroll

Odo Hirsch
Russell Stannard

The Christmas Mystery
The Frog Castle
Hello? Is Anybody There?

Jack Gantos

Family   School   Social issues

12-14

Morris Gleitzman
Jonathan Kebbe

Gene Kemp

Joey Pigza Loses Control
Joey Pigza Swallowed the Key

Leon Garfield
Adventure Historical

8-11

12-14

Melvin Burgess
Cynthia Harnett

Terry Jones
Rosemary Sutcliff

The Apprentices
Black Jack
December Rose
Devil in the Fog
John Diamond
Stolen Watch

Alan Garner
Adventure Fantasy

12-14

Mary Arrigan
Susan Cooper
Kevin Crossley-Holland
Catherine Fisher
Diana Wynne Jones

William Mayne
Philip Pullman
Enid Richemont
J R R Tolkien
T H White

A Bag of Moonshine
Elidor
The Moon of Gomrath
The Weirdstone of Brisingamen

Susan Gates
Adventure Family Fantasy Humour

5-7 12-14

Tony Bradman
Keith Brumpton

Mark Haddon
Michael Lawrence

Invasion of the Vampire Spiders
Killer Mushrooms Ate My Gran
Night of the Haunted Trousers

Don't forget: Picture Books ∗ Genres ∗ Series ∗ Book Prizes ∗ Bibliography ☞

Jamila Gavin

Family Fantasy Other lands

5-7 12-14

Mary Arrigan
Malorie Blackman
Mary Ellis
Adèle Geras

Rumer Godden
Grace Hallworth
Julia Jarman
Catherine Sefton

Danger by Moonlight
Deadly Friend
Grandpa Chatterji
Grandpa's Indian Summer
The Magic Orange Tree
Star Child on Clark Street

Adèle Geras

Ballet Family War 1939-45

5-7 12-14

Antonia Barber
Nina Bawden
Elinor M Brent-Dyer
Jamila Gavin
Rumer Godden

Mal Lewis Jones
Ann Jungman
Noel Streatfeild
Kaye Umansky

A Candle in the Dark
Good Luck Louisa
Louisa in the Wings

Alan Gibbons

Computers Fantasy Social issues Sport

12-14

Neil Arksey
Bernard Ashley
Terence Blacker
Malorie Blackman
Rob Childs

Michael Coleman
Michael Hardcastle
Diana Hendry
Celia Rees
R L Stine

Injury Time
Ganging Up
Under Pressure

Legendeer Trilogy
Total Football Series

Morris Gleitzman

Family   Humour

12-14

8-11

Roy Apps
Philip Ardagh
Jack Gantos
Mark Haddon
Harry Horse

Paul Jennings
Robin Klein
Philip Ridley
E F Smith
Nicholas Warburton

Blabbermouth
Bumface
Stickybeak
Toad Heaven
Toad Rage
Worrywarts

Debi Gliori

Family   Fantasy   Humour   Magic

Henrietta Branford
Eoin Colfer
Roald Dahl
Nigel Hinton

Michael Hoeye
Terry Pratchett
Lemony Snicket

Pure Dead Magic
Pure Dead Wicked

Rumer Godden

Family

Jamila Gavin
Adèle Geras

Elizabeth Goudge

The Diddakoi
The Doll's House

Elizabeth Goudge

Fantasy

Lynne Reid Banks
Lucy M Boston

Frances Hodgson Burnett
Rumer Godden

I Saw Three Ships
The Little White Horse

Kenneth Grahame

Animals   Fantasy

W J Corbett
Colin Dann
Brian Jacques
Tove Jansson

Dick King-Smith
Hugh Lofting
A A Milne

The Reluctant Dragon
The Wind in the Willows

Mark Haddon

Humour   Space

Steve Barlow and
   Steve Skidmore
Simon Cheshire
Bruce Coville

Susan Gates
Morris Gleitzman
Paul Jennings
Philip Ridley

Agent Z and the Killer Bananas
Agent Z and the Penguin from Mars
The Real Porky Phillips

Willis Hall

Humour

Hunter Davies
Anthony Horowitz
Eva Ibbotson
Ivan Jones
Ann Jungman

Margaret Mahy
Lemony Snicket
Angela Sommer-Bodenburg
Kaye Umansky
David Henry Wilson

The Last Vampire
The Vampire Hunt
Vampire Island

Grace Hallworth

Ghost/supernatural   Other cultures

Kevin Crossley-Holland
Mary Ellis

Jamila Gavin

Cric Crac
Listen To This Story
Mermaids and Monsters
Sing Me a Story!

72

Dennis Hamley   Det mysteries Ghost/supernat Hist'l: Vict War

Jan Mark   Jean Ure
Alison Prince

Angel's Snare
The Diary of a Young Soldier in World War I
The Diary of a Victorian Apprentice
Ryan's United

Michael Hardcastle   Sport

Neil Arksey   Alan Durant
Terence Blacker   Alan Gibbons
Tony Bradman   Paul May
Rob Childs   Martin Waddell

And Davey Must Score
Downhill Bike
Hit It

Cynthia Harnett   Historical: Medieval

Kevin Crossley-Holland   Leon Garfield
Karen Cushman   Rosemary Sutcliff

The Load of Unicorn
The Wool Pack

Elizabeth Hawkins   Adventure Animals Humour War 1939-45

5-7

Diana Hendry   Pete Johnson
Michael Hoeye   Martin Waddell

Hamster in Danger
Hamster and a Robbery
Sea of Peril

*Don't forget: Picture Books * Genres * Series * Book Prizes * Bibliography* ☞

8-11

Diana Hendry Family   Fantasy

8-11

12-14

Vivien Alcock

Helen Cresswell

Roald Dahl

Annie Dalton

Stephen Elboz

Alan Gibbons

Elizabeth Hawkins

Hilary McKay

Jill Murphy

J K Rowling

The Crazy Collector
Harvey Angell and the Ghost Child
Harvey Angell Beats Time
Minders

Douglas Hill Ghost/supernatural   Magic   Science fiction

5-7

John Christopher

Bruce Coville

Terrance Dicks

Nicholas Fisk

Maggie Prince

Alien Citadel
Alien Deeps
Meleron's Magic

Nigel Hinton Adventure   Fantasy

12-14

Debi Gliori

Russell Hoban

Mary Norton

Robert C O'Brien

The Finders

Beaver Towers Series

Odo Hirsch Adventure   Detective mysteries   Fantasy   Humour

Jostein Gaarder

Cliff McNish

William Nicholson

Stephen Potts

Bartlett and the City of Flames
Bartlett and the Ice Voyage
Hazel Green
Something's Fishy Hazel Green

Russell Hoban

Fantasy

J M Barrie
Lewis Carroll
Nigel Hinton
C S Lewis

William Mayne
Mary Norton
Robert C O'Brien

The Mouse and His Child
Ponders

8-11

Michael Hoeye

Adventure   Animals   Fantasy   Humour

Eoin Colfer
Debi Gliori
Elizabeth Hawkins
Brian Jacques

Robin Jarvis
Garry Kilworth
Dick King-Smith
E B White

Time Stops for No Mouse

Anne Holm

War 1939-45

Andrew Davies
Jackie French
Judith Kerr

Ian Serraillier
Robert Westall

I Am David

Mary Hooper

Animals   Historical   Humour   School

5-7 12-14

Beverly Cleary
Paula Danziger
Lois Lowry

Margaret Mahy
Dyan Sheldon
Jean Ure

The Lost Treasure
Mad About the Boy
Lucy's Farm Series

Don't forget: Picture Books * Genres * Series * Book Prizes * Bibliography ☞

Anthony Horowitz   Adventure   Computers   Historical   Humour

12-14

Herbie Brennan
Gillian Cross
Roald Dahl
Clive Dickinson
Willis Hall

Harry Horse
Eva Ibbotson
Paul Jennings
Philip Ridley
Ian Whybrow

The Devil and His Boy
The Falcon's Malteser
Granny
Groosham Grange
The Unholy Grail: a Tale of Groosham Grange
The Switch

Harry Horse   Letters

Clive Dickinson
Morris Gleitzman

Anthony Horowitz

The Last Cowboys
The Last Gold Diggers
The Last Polar Bears

Lesley Howarth   Computers   Environment   Fantasy   Sci fiction

12-14

Helen Dunmore
Andrew Norriss

Celia Rees

I Managed a Monster
Mister Spaceman
Paulina
Ultraviolet

Ted Hughes   Environment   Fantasy   Mythology

Melvin Burgess
Clive King

Robert C O'Brien

The Dreamfighter and Other Creation Tales
How the Whale Became and Other Stories
The Iron Man
The Iron Woman

Pat Hutchins
8-11

Adventure   Detective mysteries   Humour   School

Henrietta Branford

Rose Impey

Sheila Lavelle

Jacqueline Wilson

The Curse of the Egyptian Mummy
The House That Sailed Away

Eva Ibbotson

Adventure   Fantasy   Ghost/supernatural   Humour

12-14

Roald Dahl

Willis Hall

Anthony Horowitz

Ivan Jones

Ann Jungman

Jill Murphy

J K Rowling

Kate Saunders

Angela Sommer-Bodenburg

Kaye Umansky

The Great Ghost Rescue
The Haunting of Hiram
Journey to the River Sea
Not Just a Witch
The Secret of Platform B
Which Witch

Rose Impey

Family   Humour

5-7

Jenny Dale

Narinder Dhami

Pat Hutchins

Sheila Lavelle

Ann Pilling

Jean Ure

Jacqueline Wilson

Holly's Puppies
Houdini Dog
Starring the Sleepover Club

Brian Jacques

Adventure   Fantasy

12-14

Richard Adams

David Clement-Davies

W J Corbett

Colin Dann

Kenneth Grahame

Michael Hoeye

Tove Jansson

Robin Jarvis

Garry Kilworth

Robert C O'Brien

Redwall Series

77

Tove Jansson   Fantasy

Kenneth Grahame   A A Milne
Brian Jacques   Mary Norton

Finn Family Moomintroll

8-11

Julia Jarman   Computers Family Ghost/supernatural Historical

5-7

Malorie Blackman   Robin Kingsland
Jamila Gavin

Computer Kate
Hangman
The Haunting of Nadia
The Jessame Stories
Ollie and the Bogle
The Time-travelling Cat Series

Robin Jarvis   Fantasy

12-14

Joan Aiken   Michael Hoeye
Susan Cooper   Brian Jacques
Catherine Fisher   Cliff McNish

The Deptford Histories Series
The Whitby Witches Series

Paul Jennings   Fantasy Humour

12-14

Roy Apps   Anthony Horowitz
Bruce Coville   Philip Ridley
Richmal Crompton   Jeremy Strong
Morris Gleitzman   Nicholas Warburton
Mark Haddon   David Henry Wilson

The Gizmo
The Gizmo Again
Singenpoo's Secret Weapon
Singenpoo Shoots Through

Brenda Jobling   Animals

Lucy Daniels   Tessa Krailing
Dick King-Smith   Jenny Oldfield

The Dog with the Wounded Paw
The Kitten with the Injured Tail
The Pony with the Bandaged Ear

8-11

Pete Johnson   Ghost/supernatural Humour Thrillers

12-14

Elizabeth Hawkins   Paul Stewart
Allan Frewin Jones   R L Stine
Anthony Masters   Robert Swindells

Bug Brother
Mind Reader
The Phantom Thief
Pirate Brother
Rescuing Dad
Traitor

Allan Frewin Jones   Adventure Det mys Ghost/super Horror

Pete Johnson   Paul Stewart
Anthony Masters   Robert Swindells

Dark Paths Series

Diana Wynne Jones   Fantasy Ghost/supernat Humour Magic

12-14

Joan Aiken   Pauline Fisk
Theresa Breslin   Alan Garner
Helen Cresswell   E Nesbit
Stephen Elboz   Philip Pullman
Catherine Fisher   J K Rowling

Eight Days of Luke
A Tale of Time City
Wild Robert

Worlds of Chrestomanci Series

Ivan Jones — Ghost/supernatural Humour

Willis Hall   Eva Ibbotson

The Ghost Hunter
The Ghost Hunter at Chillwood Castle
The Ghost Hunter's House of Horror

Mal Lewis Jones — Ballet

Antonia Barber   Noel Streatfeild
Adèle Geras

Danger at the Castle
Skeleton in the Wardrobe

Terry Jones — Fantasy Historical: Medieval Mythology

Joan Aiken   Terry Pratchett
Kevin Crossley-Holland   Rosemary Sutcliff
Leon Garfield   T H White

Fairy Tales
Fantastic Stories
The Knight and the Squire
The Lady and the Squire

Ann Jungman — Fantasy Humour War 1939-45

5-7

Terry Deary   Eva Ibbotson
Adèle Geras   Angela Sommer-Bodenburg
Willis Hall

Lucy Keeps the Wolf from the Door
Resistance
Vlad the Drac

Jonathan Kebbe — Family Humour School

Jack Gantos   Nicholas Warburton
E F Smith

The Bottle-top King
Spoffer Rooney

Carolyn Keene
Adventure   Detective mysteries

Enid Blyton   Ann M Martin
Franklin W Dixon   Anthony Masters
Fiona Kelly

Nancy Drew Series

8-11

Fiona Kelly
Adventure   Detective mysteries

Franklin W Dixon   Ann M Martin
Carolyn Keene   Anthony Masters

The Mystery Club Series

Gene Kemp
Humour   School

Bernard Ashley   Astrid Lindgren
Gillian Cross   Hilary McKay
Anne Fine   Catherine MacPhail
Jack Gantos   Hazel Townson
Tessa Krailing   Nicholas Warburton

Charlie Lewis Plays for Time
Gowie Corby Plays Chicken
The Hairy Hands
The Turbulent Term of Tyke Tyler

Judith Kerr
War 1939-45

Nina Bawden   Alison Prince
Jackie French   Ian Serraillier
Anne Holm   Ann Turnbull
Michelle Magorian   Robert Westall
Linda Newberry

Bombs on Aunt Daisy
A Small Person Far Away
When Hitler Stole Pink Rabbit

Don't forget: Picture Books * Genres * Series * Book Prizes * Bibliography ☞

Garry Kilworth
Adventure   Animals   Fantasy   War

Joan Aiken
David Clement-Davies
W J Corbett

Catherine Fisher
Michael Hoeye
Brian Jacques

Drummer Boy
The Gargoyle
Night Dancer
Soldier's Son

The Welkin Weasels Series

Clive King
Adventure   Environment

David Almond
Lynne Reid Banks
Ted Hughes

Andrew Norriss
Robert C O'Brien
Arthur Ransome

Me and My Million
Stig of the Dump

Dick King-Smith
Animals   Family   Humour

5-7

Michael Bond
Lucy Daniels
Colin Dann
Kenneth Grahame
Michael Hoeye

Brenda Jobling
Hugh Lofting
Jenny Oldfield
Dodie Smith
E B White

Ace
Billy the Bird
The Crowstarver
Harry's Mad
Lady Lollipop
Magnus Powermouse
The Sheep Pig

Robin Kingsland
Adventure   Detective mysteries   Humour

Julia Jarman

Michael Lawrence

Cowardly Cutlass
Doghouse Reilly
Doghouse Reilly in Sitting Ducks
Mo and the Mummy Case

Robin Klein
Family   Ghost/supernatural   Humour   Thrillers

Judy Blume
Betsy Byars

Sharon Creech
Morris Gleitzman

All in the Blue Unclouded Weather
Gabby's Fair
Hating Alison Ashley
The List Maker

8-11

Tessa Krailing
Adventure   Animals   Family   School

5-7

Lucy Daniels
Brenda Jobling
Gene Kemp

Sheila Lavelle
Jean Ure

The Case of the Talking Trousers
The Great Dinosaur Kidnap
Message from Venus

Elizabeth Laird
Animals   Family

12-14

Gillian Cross
Lucy Daniels

Colin Dann
Michael Morpurgo

Secret Friends
Wild Things Series

Sheila Lavelle
Family   Humour

5-7

Judy Blume
Beverly Cleary
Hunter Davies
Pat Hutchins
Rose Impey

Tessa Krailing
Lois Lowry
Hilary McKay
Jill Murphy

My Best Fiend
Calamity with the Fiend
The Fiend Next Door

Don't forget: Picture Books * Genres * Series * Book Prizes * Bibliography ☞

Michael Lawrence
Fantasy   Humour

Susan Gates   Robin Kingsland

Finella Minella
The Killer Underpants
The Poltergoose
The Toilet of Doom
Young Dracula

Robert Leeson
Fantasy   Humour   School   War 1939-45

5-7 12-14

Bernard Ashley   Michael Morpurgo
Kevin Crossley-Holland   Andrew Norriss
Terry Deary   Robert Westall
Jan Mark   T H White

Lucky Lad
Smart Girls
The Song of Arthur
The Third Class Genie
Tom's Private War
Tom's War Patrol

Gail Carson Levine
Adventure   Fantasy   Humour

Laurence Anholt   Helen Cresswell
Tony Bradman   Jill Murphy

Cinderellis and the Glass Hill
Dave at Night
Ella Enchanted
The Fairy's Mistake
The Two Princesses of Bamarre

C S Lewis
Fantasy

J M Barrie   E Nesbit
Frank L Baum   Philip Pullman
Lewis Carroll   Enid Richemont
Russell Hoban   J R R Tolkien
Cliff McNish   T H White

Chronicles of Narnia

Astrid Lindgren

Adventure   Fantasy

Gene Kemp
Lois Lowry

Alf Prøysen

Pippi Goes Aboard
Pippi Longstocking
Pippi in the South Seas

8-11

Penelope Lively

Adventure   Fantasy   Ghost/supernatural

5-7 12-14

Lynne Reid Banks
Helen Cresswell
Berlie Doherty
Penelope Farmer

William Mayne
Philippa Pearce
K M Peyton
Catherine Storr

Astercote
The Ghost of Thomas Kempe
The House in Norham Gardens
A Stitch in Time

Hugh Lofting

Animals   Fantasy

Kenneth Grahame

Dick King-Smith

The Doctor Dolittle Series

Lois Lowry

Family   Fantasy   Humour   War 1939-45

12-14

Judy Blume
Betsy Byars
Paula Danziger
Mary Hooper

Sheila Lavelle
Astrid Lindgren
Jean Ure
Jacqueline Wilson

The Giver
Number the Stars
Anastasia Series

Don't forget: Picture Books * Genres * Series * Book Prizes * Bibliography ☞

Geraldine McCaughrean

Fantasy   Historical   Other lands

5-7 12-14

Lewis Carroll
Susan Cooper
Kevin Crossley-Holland

Berlie Doherty
Michael Morpurgo
Theresa Tomlinson

Casting the Gods Adrift
The Kite Rider
A Little Lower Than the Angels
A Pack of Lies
Six Storey House
Stop the Train

Hilary McKay

Family   Ghost/supernatural   Humour   Magic

5-7 12-14

Louisa May Alcott
Gillian Cross
Hunter Davies
Helen Dunmore
Anne Fine

Diana Hendry
Gene Kemp
Sheila Lavelle
Ann Pilling
Jacqueline Wilson

The Amber Cat
Dog Friday
Dolphin Luck
The Exiles
Saffy's Angel

Cliff McNish

Fantasy   Magic

Philip Ardagh
Stephen Elboz
Odo Hirsch
Robin Jarvis

C S Lewis
William Nicholson
Enid Richemont
J K Rowling

The Doomspell Trilogy

Catherine MacPhail

Det mysteries   Family   Social iss   Thrillers

12-14

Gene Kemp

Jan Mark

Fugitive
Missing
Picking on Percy

8-11

Michelle Magorian
Family   War 1939-45

12-14

Rachel Anderson
Nina Bawden
Jackie French
Judith Kerr
Linda Newberry

Philippa Pearce
Alison Prince
Ian Serraillier
Ann Turnbull
Robert Westall

Back Home
Goodnight Mister Tom
A Spoonful of Jam

Margaret Mahy
Adventure   Family   Ghost/supernat   Humour

5-7 12-14

Laurence Anholt
Willis Hall
Mary Hooper
Philip Ridley

Nicholas Warburton
Ursula Moray Williams
David Henry Wilson

The Haunting
The Riddle of the Frozen Phantom
A Villain's Night Out

Jan Mark
Family   Ghost/supernatural   Humour   School

5-7 12-14

David Almond
Bernard Ashley
Julie Bertagna
Sharon Creech
Gillian Cross

Dennis Hamley
Robert Leeson
Catherine MacPhail
Andrew Norriss

Lady with the Iron Bones
Long Lost
Nothing to Be Afraid of
Thunder and Lightnings

8-11

Don't forget: Picture Books * Genres * Series * Book Prizes * Bibliography ☞

Ann M Martin — Adventure Detective mysteries Family

Franklin W Dixon
Carolyn Keene

Fiona Kelly

Babysitters Mystery
Happy Holidays, Jessi
Kirsty's Worst Idea
Stacey's Problem
Babysitters Club Series

Anthony Masters — Adventure Ghost/supernatural

5-7 12-14

Enid Blyton
Pete Johnson
Allan Frewin Jones
Carolyn Keene

Fiona Kelly
Robert Swindells
Robert Westall

Bicycle Blues
Ghosthunters Series

Andrew Matthews — Fantasy Humour Romance

5-7

Jeremy Strong

Kaye Umansky

The G.S.O.H.
Loads of Trouble

Paul May — Sport

Neil Arksey
Rob Childs

Michael Coleman
Michael Hardcastle

Defenders
Green Fingers
Nice One, Smithy
Trouble Makers

William Mayne
Family   Fantasy   School

Alan Garner   Penelope Lively
Russell Hoban

Antar and the Eagles
Candlefasts
Cradlefasts
Earthfasts
The Worm in the Well

8-11

Anne Merrick
Adventure   Fantasy

Penelope Farmer   Philippa Pearce
Pauline Fisk   Sylvia Waugh

Hannah's Ghost
The Snow Globe
Someone Came Knocking

A A Milne
Animals

Michael Bond   Tove Jansson
Kenneth Grahame

The House at Pooh Corner
Winnie the Pooh

L M Montgomery
Family

Louisa May Alcott   Johanna Spyri
Susan M Coolidge   Laura Ingalls Wilder

Anne of Avonlea
Anne of Green Gables
Anne of the Island

Don't forget: Picture Books ∗ Genres ∗ Series ∗ Book Prizes ∗ Bibliography ☞

Michael Morpurgo   Adventure Hist'l Social iss War 1939-45

5-7 12-14

Rachel Anderson   Geraldine McCaughrean
Kevin Crossley-Holland   Jenny Nimmo
Chris d'Lacey   Philippa Pearce
Elizabeth Laird   Robert Westall
Robert Leeson   T H White

Arthur, High King of Britain
Billy the Kid
Kensuke's Kingdom
Out of the Ashes
The Sleeping Sword
Toro! Toro!

Jill Murphy   Fantasy Humour Magic

5-7

Kathryn Cave   Sheila Lavelle
Edward Eager   Gail Carson Levine
Diana Hendry   Kate Saunders
Eva Ibbotson   Kaye Umansky

Worst Witch
A Bad Spell for the Worst Witch
The Worst Witch Strikes Again

Magdalen Nabb   Det mysteries Fantasy Ghost/supernatural

5-7

Penelope Farmer   Martin Waddell
Catherine Storr   Ursula Moray Williams

The Enchanted Horse
Twilight Ghost

E Nesbit   Family Fantasy

Lynne Reid Banks   C S Lewis
Lucy M Boston   Philip Pullman
Frances Hodgson Burnett   Enid Richemont
Edward Eager   Sylvia Waugh
Diana Wynne Jones

Five Children and It
The Phoenix and the Carpet
The Railway Children

Linda Newberry

12-14

Nina Bawden
Berlie Doherty
Judith Kerr

Michelle Magorian
K M Peyton

Blitz Boys
Flightsend
Ice Cat

William Nicholson
Adventure   Fantasy

12-14

Joan Aiken
Susan Cooper
Annie Dalton

Odo Hirsch
Cliff McNish

Firesong
Slaves of the Mastery
The Wind Singer

Jenny Nimmo
Family   Fantasy   Ghost/supernat   Science fiction

5-7 12-14

Vivien Alcock
Mary Arrigan
Melvin Burgess
Susan Cooper
Catherine Fisher

Michael Morpurgo
Stephen Potts
Philip Pullman
Enid Richemont
J K Rowling

Dog Star
Emlyn's Moon
Griffin's Castle
Milo's Wolves
The Owl Tree
The Snow Spider

Andrew Norriss
Family   Fantasy   Humour   Science fiction

David Almond
Lesley Howarth
Clive King

Robert Leeson
Jan Mark

Aquila
Bernard's Watch
Matt's Million

91

Mary Norton

8-11

Adventure Family Fantasy

Lynne Reid Banks
Nigel Hinton
Russell Hoban
Tove Jansson

Alf Prøysen
P L Travers
Sylvia Waugh

Bedknob and Broomstick
The Borrowers
The Borrowers Afield
The Borrowers Afloat
The Borrowers Aloft

Robert C O'Brien

Environment Fantasy

12-14

Nigel Hinton
Russell Hoban
Ted Hughes

Brian Jacques
Clive King

Mrs Frisby and the Rats of Nimh
The Silver Crown

Jenny Oldfield

Animals Humour Pony/horse

5-7

Bernard Ashley
Emily Costello
Jenny Dale
Lucy Daniels

Colin Dann
Wendy Douthwaite
Brenda Jobling
Dick King-Smith

Eagle Wing
Mac Climbs a Mountain
Maisy Wants Her Mum
Moondance
Home Farm Twins Series
Horses of Half Moon Ranch Series

Katherine Paterson

Family Other lands Social issues

12-14

Sharon Creech
Kate di Camillo

Berlie Doherty

Bridge to Terabithia
The Great Gilly Hopkins

Gary Paulsen

12-14

Roy Apps
Melvin Burgess

Chris d'Lacey

Christmas Sonata
Nightjohn
Sarny
Video Trap

8-11

Philippa Pearce

Adventure Animals Family Fantasy

Lucy M Boston
Helen Cresswell
Berlie Doherty
Penelope Farmer
Penelope Lively

Michelle Magorian
Anne Merrick
Michael Morpurgo
Arthur Ransome
Alison Uttley

The Battle of Bubble and Squeak
A Dog So Small
Minnow on the Say
The Rope and Other Stories
Tom's Midnight Garden
The Way to Sattin Shore

K M Peyton

Pony/horse Thrillers

5-7 12-14

Enid Bagnold
Wendy Douthwaite
Penelope Lively

Linda Newberry
Anna Sewell

Blind Beauty
A Midsummer Night's Death
A Pattern of Roses
Prove Yourself a Hero
Stealaway

Helena Pielichaty

Diaries Family Letters School

12-14

Malorie Blackman
Paula Danziger

Anne Fine
Frances Thomas

Simone's Diary
Simone's Letters
Simone's Website
There's Only One Danny Ogle
Vicious Circle

Ann Pilling
Family　Fantasy　Horror　Humour

5-7

Rose Impey　　　　　　　Jacqueline Wilson
Hilary McKay

Black Harvest
Henry's Leg
The Pit
The Witch of Lagg

8-11

Stephen Potts
Adventure　Fantasy

12-14

David Almond　　　　　　Jenny Nimmo
Odo Hirsch

Compass Murphy
Hunting Gumnor
Tommy Trouble

Terry Pratchett
Fantasy

12-14

Eoin Colfer　　　　　　Terry Jones
Debi Gliori　　　　　　Philip Ridley

The Amazing Maurice and His Educated Rodents
The Carpet People
Diggers
Only You Can Save Mankind
Truckers
Wings

Susan Price
Fantasy　Ghost/supernatural

12-14

David Almond　　　　　　Celia Rees
Annie Dalton

Elf King
Foiling the Dragon
The Ghost Drum
Ghost Song
Hairy Bill
Telling Tales

Alison Prince   Family   Ghost/supernat   Historical   War 1939-45

5-7 12-14

Rachel Anderson

Dennis Hamley

Judith Kerr

Michelle Magorian

Catherine Sefton

Ann Turnbull

Martin Waddell

8-11

A Story About the ... Acts of Union: a Nation Again
How's Business
Second Chance
The Sherwood Hero
My Tudor Queen

Maggie Prince   Ghost/supernat   Science fiction   War 1939-45

John Christopher

Nicholas Fisk

Douglas Hill

Russell Stannard

Here Comes a Candle to Light You to Bed
How's Business
Memoirs of a Dangerous Alien
Pulling the Plug on the Universe

Alf Prøysen   Magic

5-7

Astrid Lindgren   Mary Norton

Mrs Pepperpot Stories

Philip Pullman   Adventure   Fantasy

12-14

Joan Aiken

Susan Cooper

Catherine Fisher

Alan Garner

Diana Wynne Jones

C S Lewis

E Nesbit

Jenny Nimmo

Kate Thompson

J R R Tolkien

Clockwork: or All Wound Up
Count Karlstein, or the Ride of the Demon Huntsman
The Firework-maker's Daughter
The Gas-fitters Ball
I Was a Rat! or the Scarlet Slippers
His Dark Materials Trilogy

Arthur Ransome

Adventure   Family

Enid Blyton
Gillian Cross

Clive King
Philippa Pearce

Coot Club
Great Northern
Missee Lee
Peter Duck
Pigeon Post
Swallows and Amazons

8-11

Celia Rees

Fantasy   Ghost/supernatural   Social issues

12-14

Joan Aiken
Alan Gibbons

Lesley Howarth
Susan Price

The Bailey Game
The Cunning Man
Soul Taker
A Trap in Time

Enid Richemont

Fantasy   Ghost/supernatural   Science fiction

Theresa Breslin
Alan Garner
C S Lewis

Cliff McNish
E Nesbit
Jenny Nimmo

Dream Dog
Enchanted Village
To Summon a Spirit

Philip Ridley

Family   Fantasy   Humour

12-14

Philip Ardagh
Eoin Colfer
Roald Dahl
Morris Gleitzman
Mark Haddon

Anthony Horowitz
Paul Jennings
Margaret Mahy
Terry Pratchett
Lemony Snicket

Kaspar in the Glitter
Krindle Krax
Mighty Fizz Chilla
Vinegar Street
Zinder Zunder

J K Rowling

Fantasy Magic School

12-14

Theresa Breslin
Annie Dalton
Stephen Elboz
Catherine Fisher
Diana Hendry

Eva Ibbotson
Diana Wynne Jones
Cliff McNish
Jenny Nimmo
Kaye Umansky

8-11

Harry Potter and the Chamber of Secrets
Harry Potter and the Goblet of Fire
Harry Potter and the Philosopher's Stone
Harry Potter and the Prisoner of Azkaban

Kate Saunders

Fantasy

Terence Blacker
Eva Ibbotson

Jill Murphy

The Belfry Witches Series

Catherine Sefton

Adventure Ghost/supernatural

is Martin Waddell

5-7

Jamila Gavin
Alison Prince

Ann Turnbull

The Haunting of Ellen
In a Blue Velvet Dress

Ian Serraillier

War 1939-45

Jackie French
Anne Holm
Judith Kerr

Michelle Magorian
Robert Westall

The Silver Sword

Anna Sewell

Animals Pony/horse

Enid Bagnold
Lucy Daniels

K M Peyton

Black Beauty

97

Dyan Sheldon

Adventure   Humour

5-7 12-14

Paula Danziger   Mary Hooper

Harry the Explorer
Lizzie and Charlie Go Shopping
Lizzie and Charlie Go to the Movies
Ride on Sister Vincent

Francesca Simon

Family   Humour

5-7

Laurence Anholt   Jean Ure
Paula Danziger   David Henry Wilson

The Horrid Henry Series

Dodie Smith

Adventure   Animals

Colin Dann   E B White
Dick King-Smith

One Hundred and One Dalmations

E F Smith

Family   Humour

also writes as Emily Smith

Sharon Creech   Jonathan Kebbe
Morris Gleitzman

What Howls at the Moon in Frilly Knickers

Lemony Snicket

Fantasy   Humour

12-14

Philip Ardagh   Willis Hall
Thomas Bloor   Philip Ridley
Roald Dahl   R L Stine
Debi Gliori

A Series of Unfortunate Events Series

Angela Sommer-Bodenburg Humour

Willis Hall
Eva Ibbotson

Ann Jungman
Kaye Umansky

The Little Vampire
The Little Vampire and the Wicked Plot
The Little Vampire Gets a Surprise

8-11

Johanna Spyri Family

Louisa May Alcott
Susan M Coolidge

L M Montgomery
Laura Ingalls Wilder

Heidi

Russell Stannard Adventure   School   Space

Steve Barlow and
   Steve Skidmore
Nicholas Fisk

Jostein Gaarder
Maggie Prince

Black Holes and Uncle Albert
Dr Dyer's Academy
The Time and Space of Uncle Albert
Uncle Albert and the Quantum Quest
World of 1001 Mysteries

Paul Stewart Animals   Fantasy   Ghost/supernatural   Sport

5-7

Mary Arrigan
Melvin Burgess
Pete Johnson

Allan Frewin Jones
R L Stine
Robert Swindells

Football Mad
The Midnight Hand
The Edge Chronicles Series

Don't forget: Picture Books * Genres * Series * Book Prizes * Bibliography ☞

8-11

R L Stine
Computers Horror

12-14

Nicholas Fisk
Alan Gibbons
Pete Johnson

Lemony Snicket
Paul Stewart

It Came from the Internet
The Nightmare Room
Shop Till You Drop ... Dead!

Catherine Storr
Fantasy Ghost/supernatural

Allan Ahlberg
Joan Aiken
Mary Arrigan
Helen Cresswell
Penelope Farmer

Pauline Fisk
Penelope Lively
Magdalen Nabb
Ursula Moray Williams

Clever Polly and the Stupid Wolf
The If Game
Marianne Dreams
The Mirror Image Ghost

Noel Streatfeild
Ballet Family Stage War 1939-45

Antonia Barber
Adèle Geras

Mal Lewis Jones

Ballet Shoes
Ballet Shoes for Anna
When the Siren Wailed

Jeremy Strong
Computers Family Humour

5-7

Allan Ahlberg
Roy Apps
Tony Bradman
Henrietta Branford
Simon Cheshire

Paul Jennings
Andrew Matthews
Hazel Townson
Ian Whybrow
David Henry Wilson

The Hundred-mile-an-hour Dog
Krazy Kow Saves the World - Well Almost
Mad Iris
My Mum's Going to Explode
Sir Rupert and Rosie Gusset in Deadly Danger
Viking at School

Rosemary Sutcliff
Historical: Medieval / Roman   Mythology

12-14

Kevin Crossley-Holland
Karen Cushman
Leon Garfield
Cynthia Harnett

Terry Jones
Theresa Tomlinson
T H White

Beowulf: Dragonslayer
Black Ships Before Troy
The High Deeds of Finn MacCool
King Arthur Stories
The Eagle of the Ninth Sequence

8-11

Robert Swindells
Adventure Ghost/super Sci fiction War '39-45

5-7 12-14

Thomas Bloor
Pete Johnson
Allan Frewin Jones
Anthony Masters

Paul Stewart
Kate Thompson
Robert Westall

Blitzed
Invisible!
Jacqueline Hyde
Room 13
The Thousand Eyes of Night
Timesnatch

Ruth Symes
Family   Social issues

Judy Blume

Betsy Byars

Frankie's Romeo
The Mum Trap

Alan Temperley
Adventure Fantasy Humour Magic

Roy Apps
Theresa Breslin

Keith Brumpton

The Brave Whale
Harry and the Wrinklies
Ragboy Rats and the Surging Sea
The Simple Giant

Frances Thomas

Diaries   Family

Beverly Cleary   Ian Whybrow
Helena Pielichaty

Polly's Absolutely Worst Birthday Ever
Polly's Running Away Book

Kate Thompson

Fantasy   Ghost/supernatural

12-14

Malorie Blackman   Robert Swindells
Philip Pullman

The Beguilers
The Switchers Trilogy

J R R Tolkien

Adventure   Fantasy

12-14

Susan Cooper   C S Lewis
Alan Garner   Philip Pullman

The Hobbit
The Lord of the Rings

Theresa Tomlinson

Family   Fantasy   Historical   Social issues

5-7   12-14

Henrietta Branford   Rosemary Sutcliff
Geraldine McCaughrean

Beneath Burning Mountain
Child of the May
Dancing Through the Shadows
The Voyage of the Silver Bream

Hazel Townson

Detective mysteries   Family   Humour

Allan Ahlberg   Jeremy Strong
Anne Fine   David Henry Wilson
Gene Kemp

Ignorance is Bliss
The Invisible Boy
Your Dad and My Mum
Lenny and Jake Series

P L Travers

8-11

Family   Fantasy   Humour   Magic

J M Barrie
Frank L Baum
Lucy M Boston

Lewis Carroll
Mary Norton

Mary Poppins
Mary Poppins Comes Back
Mary Poppins in Cherry Tree Lane
Mary Poppins Opens the Door

Ann Turnbull

Family   Fantasy   Historical   War 1939-45

Nina Bawden
Jackie French
Judith Kerr
Michelle Magorian

Alison Prince
Catherine Sefton
Martin Waddell
Robert Westall

House of Ghosts
A Long Way Home
No Friend of Mine
Pigeon Summer
Room for a Stranger
The Serpent's Cave

Kaye Umansky

Humour   Magic

5-7

Edward Eager
Adèle Geras
Willis Hall
Eva Ibbotson
Andrew Matthews

Jill Murphy
J K Rowling
Angela Sommer-Bodenburg
Jean Ure
David Henry Wilson

Big Iggy
Wilma's Wicked Revenge
Pongwiffy Series

Don't forget: Picture Books * Genres * Series * Book Prizes * Bibliography ☞

Jean Ure
Diaries   Ghost/supernatural   Letters   School

5-7 12-14

Bernard Ashley
Anthony Buckeridge
Dennis Hamley
Mary Hooper
Rose Impey

Tessa Krailing
Lois Lowry
Francesca Simon
Kaye Umansky
Jacqueline Wilson

Becky Bananas: This is Your Life
Family Fan Club
Fruit and Nutcase
Shrinking Violet
Skinny Melon and Me
A Twist in Time
Sandy Simmons Series

Alison Uttley
Fantasy   Historical

5-7

Lucy M Boston
Frances Hodgson Burnett

Penelope Farmer
Philippa Pearce

A Traveller in Time

Martin Waddell
Family   Ghost/supernatural   Sport   War

also writes as Catherine Sefton

5-7 12-14

Terence Blacker
Keith Brumpton
Rob Childs
Michael Hardcastle

Elizabeth Hawkins
Magdalen Nabb
Alison Prince
Ann Turnbull

Cup Final Kid
Frankie's Story
The Ghost in the Blue Velvet Dress
The Haunting of Ellen
Napper Goes for Goal
Napper's Luck

Don't forget: Picture Books * Genres * Series * Book Prizes * Bibliography ☞

Nicholas Warburton
Adventure Humour School

Morris Gleitzman
Paul Jennings
Jonathan Kebbe

Gene Kemp
Margaret Mahy

Lost in Africa
Normal Nesbitt: the Abnormally Average Boy
The Strange Change of Flora Young
You've Been Noodled

Sylvia Waugh
Adventure Fantasy Space

12-14

Lynne Reid Banks
J M Barrie
Lucy M Boston

Anne Merrick
E Nesbit
Mary Norton

Space Race
The Mennyms Series

Robert Westall
Adventure Ghost/supernatural War 1939-45

12-14

Jackie French
Anne Holm
Judith Kerr
Robert Leeson
Michelle Magorian

Anthony Masters
Michael Morpurgo
Ian Serraillier
Robert Swindells
Ann Turnbull

Blitz
The Creature in the Dark
The Machine Gunners
Stormsearch
A Time of Fire

E B White
Animals Fantasy

Michael Hoeye
Dick King-Smith

Dodie Smith
Ursula Moray Williams

Charlotte's Web
Stuart Little

8-11

T H White

Fantasy   Mythology

Susan Cooper
Kevin Crossley-Holland
Alan Garner
Terry Jones

Robert Leeson
C S Lewis
Michael Morpurgo
Rosemary Sutcliff

The Sword in the Stone

Ian Whybrow

Diaries   Humour   Letters

5-7

Simon Cheshire
Roald Dahl
Anthony Horowitz

Jeremy Strong
Frances Thomas

Little Wolf's Book of Badness
Little Wolf's Diary of Daring Deeds
Little Wolf, Forest Detective
Little Wolf, Pack Leader

Laura Ingalls Wilder

Family   Other lands

Louisa May Alcott
Susan M Coolidge

L M Montgomery
Johanna Spyri

The Little House in the Big Woods
The Little House on the Prairie
On the Banks of Plum Creek

Ursula Moray Williams

Adventure   Animals   Fantasy

Margaret Mahy
Magdalen Nabb

Catherine Storr
E B White

Adventures of the Little Wooden Horse
Gobbolino: the Witch's Cat
Spid

David Henry Wilson

Humour

5-7

8-11

Allan Ahlberg	Margaret Mahy
Keith Brumpton	Francesca Simon
Simon Cheshire	Jeremy Strong
Willis Hall	Hazel Townson
Paul Jennings	Kaye Umansky

Elephants Don't Sit on Cars
Getting Rich with Jeremy James
Never Say Moo to a Bull
Never Steal Wheels from a Dog

Jacqueline Wilson

Family   Humour   Social issues

5-7 12-14

Judy Blume	Rose Impey
Beverly Cleary	Lois Lowry
Gillian Cross	Hilary McKay
Anne Fine	Ann Pilling
Pat Hutchins	Jean Ure

The Cat Mummy
The Dare Game
Secrets
Sleepovers
The Suitcase Kid
Tracy Beaker

Don't forget: Picture Books * Genres * Series * Book Prizes * Bibliography ☞

Authors for Ages 12-14

12-14

Yinka Adebayo — School   Social issues

Bernard Ashley
Nigel Hinton

S E Hinton
Walter Dean Myers

Drummond Hill Crew Series

Joan Aiken — Adventure   Fantasy   Ghost/supernatural   Historical

8-11

Vivien Alcock
Louise Cooper
William Corlett
Lois Duncan
Ann Halam

Robin Jarvis
Diana Wynne Jones
Penelope Lively
Hugh Scott

A Bundle of Nerves
A Creepy Company
Is

The Wolves of Willoughby Chase Series
James III Series

Vivien Alcock — Fantasy   Ghost/supernatural   Science fiction

8-11

Joan Aiken
Gillian Cross
Lois Duncan
John Gordon

Ann Halam
Anthony Horowitz
Hugh Scott
Lemony Snicket

Ghostly Companions
The Monster Garden
The Stonewalkers
Ticket to Heaven
Time Wreck

Judy Allen — Fantasy   Other lands   Social issues

5-7

Sharon Creech
Anita Desai
Paula Fox

Rosa Guy
Marcus Sedgwick

The Burning
Lord of the Dance
Stones of the Moon

David Almond
Family   Fantasy   Ghost/supernatural   Social issues

8-11

Tim Bowler
Marita Conlon-McKenna
Jostein Gaarder
Alan Garner
Sandra Glover

Pat Moon
Susan Price
Louis Sachar
Marcus Sedgwick
Sonya Sones

Counting Stars
Heaven Eyes
Kit's Wilderness
Secret Heart
Skellig

12-14

Rachel Anderson
Family   Historical   Social issues   War

5-7 8-11

Theresa Breslin
Sandra Glover
Ann Halam
Frances Mary Hendry
Christa Laird

Michelle Magorian
Michael Morpurgo
Miriam Pressler
Alison Prince
Stewart Ross

Paper Faces
Warlands

Moving Times Trilogy

K A Applegate
Fantasy   Science fiction

Louise Cooper
William Corlett
Alan Gibbons
Rhiannon Lassiter
Louise Lawrence

William Nicholson
Chloë Rayban
Gillian Rubinstein
Kate Thompson

Animorphs Series
Everworld Series

Neil Arksey
Sport

8-11

Narinder Dhami
Alan Durant

Alan Gibbons

Brooksie
Playing on the Edge
Sudden Death

109

Bernard Ashley — Family   Social issues   War

8-11

Yinka Adebayo
Veronica Bennett
Berlie Doherty
Anne Fine
Alan Gibbons

Julie Johnston
Robert Leeson
Catherine MacPhail
Jan Mark
Malcolm Rose

Little Soldier
Playing Against the Odds
Revenge House
Tiger Without Teeth
City Limits Series

Ros Asquith — Family   Humour   Romance   School

Steve Barlow and
     Steve Skidmore
Yvonne Coppard
Paula Danziger
Josephine Feeney

Elizabeth Honey
Chloë Rayban
Louise Rennison
Moya Simons
Jean Ure

Bad Hair Day
Keep Fat Class
Unbridled Passion

The Teenage Worrier Guides Series

Natalie Babbitt — Family   Fantasy

Katherine Paterson
Philip Pullman

Sylvia Waugh

Tuck Everlasting

Lynne Reid Banks — Other cultures   Other lands   Social issues

8-11

Farrukh Dhondy
Joan Lingard
Bel Mooney

Beverley Naidoo
James Watson
Sylvia Waugh

Angela and Diabola
Broken Bridge
One More River

Steve Barlow and Steve Skidmore
Diaries Fantasy Humour

8-11

Ros Asquith
Paula Danziger
Josephine Feeney

Elizabeth Honey
Louise Rennison
Sue Townsend

Dream On!
In Love with an Urban Gorilla
Whizzard
Lost Diaries Series

Nina Bawden
Family   Social issues

8-11

Tim Bowler
Theresa Breslin
Marita Conlon-McKenna
Sharon Creech
Adèle Geras

Rosa Guy
Ruth Elwin Harris
Penelope Lively
Michelle Magorian
K M Peyton

Grannie the Pag
Off the Road
The Real Plato Jones

David Belbin
Adventure   Thrillers

Malorie Blackman
Dennis Hamley
Anthony Horowitz

Gary Paulsen
Celia Rees
Malcolm Rose

Harpies
The Beat Series

Veronica Bennett
Romance   School   Social issues

Bernard Ashley
Judy Blume
Anne Fine

Pete Johnson
Brian Keaney
Robert Leeson

The Boy-free Zone
Dandelion and Bobcat
Fish Feet
Monkey

James Berry

Other cultures   Other lands

Anita Desai
Kate Elizabeth Ernest

Beverley Naidoo
James Watson

The Future-telling Lady
A Thief in the Village

Julie Bertagna

Fantasy   Social issues

8-11

Terence Blacker
Melvin Burgess
Anne Fine
Adèle Geras

Margaret Haddix
Lesley Howarth
Catherine MacPhail
Celia Rees

Exodus
Soundtrack
Spark Gap

Terence Blacker

Computers   Science fiction   Social issues

5-7 8-11

Julie Bertagna
Malorie Blackman

Jenny Nimmo

The Angel Factory
Homebird

Malorie Blackman

Computers   Family   Social issues   Thrillers

5-7 8-11

David Belbin
Terence Blacker
Peter Dickinson
Pete Johnson
Walter Dean Myers

Helena Pielichaty
Chloë Rayban
Celia Rees
Jacqueline Roy

Deadly Dare
Hacker
Pig-heart Boy
Tell Me No Lies

Don't forget: Picture Books * Genres * Series * Book Prizes * Bibliography ☞

12-14

Gary Blackwood — Adventure Historical: Tudor

Susan Cooper
Penelope Lively

Miriam Pressler

Shakespeare's Scribe
The Shakespeare Stealer

Judy Blume — Family Letters Romance Social issues

8-11

12-14

Veronica Bennett
Yvonne Coppard
Paula Danziger
Josephine Feeney

Morris Gleitzman
Helena Pielichaty
Rosie Rushton
Jacqueline Wilson

Forever
Letters to Judy
Tiger Eyes

Martin Booth — Thrillers War 1914-18 War 1939-45

Michael Morpurgo
Linda Newberry
James Riordan

Robert Swindells
Robert Westall

Music on the Bamboo Radio
Panther
P.O.W.
War Dog

Tim Bowler — Family Social issues

David Almond
Nina Bawden
Brian Keaney

Linda Newberry
Katherine Paterson

Midget
River Boy
Shadows
Storm Catchers

Henrietta Branford

Animals   Environment   Historical

5-7 8-11

Karen Cushman
Jamila Gavin
Dennis Hamley
Janni Howker
Elizabeth Laird

Geraldine McCaughrean
Rosemary Sutcliff
Theresa Tomlinson
Jill Paton Walsh

The Fated Sky
Fire, Bed and Bone
White Wolf

Theresa Breslin

Family   Fantasy   Social issues   War 1914-18

5-7 8-11

Rachel Anderson
Nina Bawden
Sharon Creech
Berlie Doherty

Michelle Magorian
Linda Newberry
Kit Pearson
Jill Paton Walsh

Death or Glory Boys
Remembrance
Whispers in the Graveyard

Melvin Burgess

Environment   Social issues   Thrillers

8-11

Julie Bertagna
Robert Cormier
Keith Gray
S E Hinton

Janni Howker
Angela Johnson
Catherine MacPhail
Gary Paulsen

An Angel for May
The Baby and Fly Pie
Billy Elliot
The Cry of the Wolf
Loving April

Eoin Colfer

Fantasy   Thrillers

8-11

Anthony Horowitz
Terry Pratchett
Philip Ridley

J K Rowling
Lemony Snicket

The Wish List
Artemis Fowl Series

Marita Conlon-McKenna Historical Other cultures War '39-45

David Almond
Nina Bawden
Lois Lowry
Elizabeth Lutzeier

Michelle Magorian
Michael Morpurgo
Kit Pearson

In Deep Dark Wood
Children of the Famine Trilogy

Louise Cooper Fantasy Science fiction

Joan Aiken
K A Applegate
Margaret Haddix

Lesley Howarth
Louise Lawrence
Lois Lowry

The Dark Caller
Daughter of Storms
Mirror, Mirror Series

12-14

Susan Cooper Adventure Fantasy Historical: Tudor

8-11

Gary Blackwood
Catherine Fisher
Leon Garfield
Alan Garner
Robin Jarvis

Ursula Le Guin
Tamora Pierce
Katherine Roberts
Rosemary Sutcliff
J R R Tolkien

King of Shadows
The Dark is Rising Series

Yvonne Coppard Diaries Family Humour

Ros Asquith
Judy Blume
Paula Danziger
Helen Dunmore
Josephine Feeney

Mary Hooper
Louise Rennison
Rosie Rushton
Moya Simons
Jacqueline Wilson

Everybody Else Does! Why Can't I?
Great! You've Just Ruined the Rest of my Life!
Hide and Seek

William Corlett
Fantasy

Joan Aiken
K A Applegate
Stephen Elboz
Lesley Howarth

Brian Jacques
Robin Jarvis
J K Rowling
Kate Thompson

The Magician's House Quartet

12-14

Robert Cormier
Horror   Romance   Social issues   Thrillers

Melvin Burgess
Lois Duncan
Pat Moon
James Riordan

Malcolm Rose
James Watson
Benjamin Zephaniah

After the First Death
The Chocolate War
Heroes
The Rag and Bone Shop
Tenderness
We All Fall Down

Sharon Creech
Adventure   Diaries   Family

8-11

Judy Allen
Nina Bawden
Theresa Breslin
Gillian Cross
Carol Hedges

Michelle Magorian
Katherine Paterson
Nicky Singer
Sonya Sones
Jerry Spinelli

Absolutely Normal Chaos
Bloomability
Chasing Redbird
Ruby Holler
Walk Two Moons
The Wanderer

Don't forget: Picture Books ∗ Genres ∗ Series ∗ Book Prizes ∗ Bibliography ☞

Gillian Cross

Adventure   School   Social issues   Thrillers

5-7 8-11

Vivien Alcock
Sharon Creech
Alan Gibbons
Eva Ibbotson
Brian Keaney

Elizabeth Laird
Geraldine McCaughrean
Jan Mark
Katherine Paterson
Jean Ure

Born of the Sun
Calling a Dead Man
Chartbreak
Dark Behind the Curtain
A Map of Nowhere
Tightrope

12-14

Kevin Crossley-Holland

Historical   Mythology

8-11

Robert Leeson
Michael Morpurgo

Rosemary Sutcliff

Arthur: at the Crossing-places
Arthur: the Seeing Stone

Karen Cushman

Historical: Medieval

8-11

Henrietta Branford
Dennis Hamley
Catherine R Johnson

Susan Price
Marcus Sedgwick
Theresa Tomlinson

Catherine, Called Birdy
Matilda Bone
The Midwife's Apprentice

Chris d'Lacey

Humour   Letters   Romance

5-7 8-11

Paula Danziger
Josephine Feeney

Mary Hooper

Falling for Mandy
From E to You

Annie Dalton

8-11

Lois Duncan
Catherine Fisher
Susan Gates

Lesley Howarth
Anthony Masters
Philip Pullman

Night Maze
Winging It
The Afterdark Series

12-14

Paula Danziger

Computers Humour Letters Romance

8-11

Ros Asquith
Steve Barlow and
   Steve Skidmore
Judy Blume
Yvonne Coppard
Chris d'Lacey

Helen Dunmore
Josephine Feeney
Mary Hooper
Rosie Rushton
Jacqueline Wilson

Can You Sue Your Parents for Malpractice?
The Divorce Express
PS Longer Letter Later: a Novel in Letters
Snail Mail No More

Anita Desai

Other lands

Judy Allen
James Berry
Jamila Gavin

Frances Mary Hendry
Suzanne Fisher Staples

The Village by the Sea

Narinder Dhami

Family Social issues Sport

8-11

Neil Arksey
Anne Fine
Elaine Forrestal
Alan Gibbons

Elizabeth Honey
Bali Rai
Jacqueline Wilson

Annie's Game
Bend It Like Beckham

Farrukh Dhondy
Other cultures   Social issues

Lynne Reid Banks
Nancy Farmer

Elizabeth Laird
Benjamin Zephaniah

Run

Peter Dickinson
Adventure   Fantasy   Ghost/supernat   Social issues

Malorie Blackman
Jostein Gaarder
Geraldine McCaughrean
Anthony Masters
William Nicholson

Gary Paulsen
Sally Prue
Philip Pullman
Kate Thompson
Robert Westall

AK
Eva
The Lion Tamer's Daughter
The Ropemaker
The Changes Trilogy
The Kin Series

Berlie Doherty
Family   Fantasy   Historical   Social issues

8-11

Bernard Ashley
Theresa Breslin
Adèle Geras
Sandra Glover
Brian Keaney

Robert Leeson
Geraldine McCaughrean
Hilary McKay
Pat Moon
Martin Waddell

Daughter of the Sea
Dear Nobody
Holly Starcross
The Snake-stone
Street Child

Malachy Doyle
Social issues

5-7

Dennis Hamley

Geraldine McCaughrean

Georgie
Who is Jesse Flood?

Lois Duncan Horror   Thrillers

Joan Aiken
Vivien Alcock
Robert Cormier
Annie Dalton

Margaret Haddix
Ann Halam
Margaret Mahy
Hugh Scott

Daughters of Eve
Don't Look Behind You
Gallows Hill
Stranger with my Face

Helen Dunmore Computers Family Romance

5-7 8-11

Yvonne Coppard
Paula Danziger
Anne Fine

Sonya Sones
Sue Welford

Brother Brother, Sister Sister
Fatal Error
Going to Egypt
Zillah and Me
The Zillah Rebellion

Alan Durant Social issues Sport Thrillers

5-7 8-11

Neil Arksey
Alan Gibbons
Paul Jennings

Pete Johnson
Anthony Masters
Sue Welford

Blood
Publish or Die

Leggs United Series

Stephen Elboz Fantasy Magic

8-11

William Corlett
Diana Hendry
Diana Wynne Jones
Ursula Le Guin

Stephen Moore
Tamora Pierce
J K Rowling
J R R Tolkien

A Land Without Magic
A Store of Secrets [originally published as *The Byzantium Bazaar*]
A Wild Kind of Magic

Deborah Ellis

Other cultures   Other lands   War

Nancy Farmer
Frances Mary Hendry
Gaye Hiçyilmaz

Elizabeth Laird
Beverley Naidoo
Suzanne Fisher Staples

The Breadwinner

Kate Elizabeth Ernest

Family   Other lands

James Berry
Virginia Hamilton

Errol Lloyd
Beverley Naidoo

Birds in the Wilderness
Festus and Felix
Hope Leaves Jamaica

12-14

Nancy Farmer

Other cultures   War

Farrukh Dhondy
Deborah Ellis
Jamila Gavin

Gaye Hiçyilmaz
Beverley Naidoo

The Ear, the Eye and the Arm
A Girl Named Disaster

Josephine Feeney

Family   School

Ros Asquith
Steve Barlow and
   Steve Skidmore
Judy Blume
Yvonne Coppard

Chris d'Lacey
Paula Danziger
Helena Pielichaty
Louise Rennison
Rosie Rushton

The Day My Parents Ran Away
My Family and Other Natural Disasters
Truth, Lies and Homework

Don't forget: Picture Books * Genres * Series * Book Prizes * Bibliography ☞

121

12-14

Anne Fine
Family   Humour   School   Social issues

5-7 8-11

Bernard Ashley
Veronica Bennett
Julie Bertagna
Narinder Dhami
Helen Dunmore

Carol Hedges
Julie Johnston
Robert Leeson
Helena Pielichaty
Jacqueline Wilson

Flour Babies
Madame Doubtfire
Step by Wicked Step
The Tulip Touch
Up on Cloud Nine

Catherine Fisher
Fantasy   Horror   Thrillers

8-11

Susan Cooper
Annie Dalton
Alan Garner
Margaret Haddix

Robin Jarvis
Diana Wynne Jones
Louise Lawrence
Ursula Le Guin

Corbenic
Darkwater Hall
The Lammas Field
The Relic Master

The Book of the Crow Series

Elaine Forrestal
Family   Other lands   Social issues

Narinder Dhami
Morris Gleitzman

Louis Sachar
Nicky Singer

Graffiti on the Fence
Someone Like Me

Paula Fox
Other lands   Social issues

Judy Allen
Julie Johnston

Cynthia Voigt

The Gathering Darkness
Monkey Island

Jostein Gaarder

Fantasy (Philosophy)

8-11

David Almond
Peter Dickinson

Alan Garner
Ursula Le Guin

Hello? Is Anybody There?
Sophie's World
Through a Glass, Darkly

Jack Gantos

Family   School   Social issues

8-11

12-14

Helena Pielichaty

Louis Sachar

Joey Pigza Loses Control
Joey Pigza Swallowed the Key

Leon Garfield

Ghost/supernatural   Historical

8-11

Susan Cooper
Catherine R Johnson
Alison Prince

Hugh Scott
Rosemary Sutcliff
Jill Paton Walsh

Jack Holborn
Revolutions
Smith
The Wedding Ghost

Alan Garner

Fantasy

8-11

David Almond
Susan Cooper
Catherine Fisher
Jostein Gaarder
John Gordon

Diana Wynne Jones
Susan Price
Sally Prue
Philip Pullman

The Owl Service
Red Shift
Stone Book Quartet

Don't forget: Picture Books * Genres * Series * Book Prizes * Bibliography ☞

Susan Gates
Fantasy   Historical   Other cultures

5-7 8-11

Annie Dalton
Margaret Mahy

Anthony Masters
Stephen Potts

Iron Heads
Pagans
Raider
White Stranger

Jamila Gavin
Historical   Other lands   Science fiction   Social issues

5-7 8-11

Henrietta Branford
Anita Desai
Nancy Farmer
Frances Mary Hendry
Miriam Pressler

Alison Prince
Bali Rai
Suzanne Fisher Staples
Mildred D Taylor

Coram Boy
Wormholers
Surya Trilogy

Jean Craighead George
Adventure   Other lands

Eva Ibbotson

Michael Morpurgo

Julie
Julie of the Wolves
My Side of the Mountain

Adèle Geras
Family   Historical   Social issues

5-7 8-11

Nina Bawden
Julie Bertagna
Berlie Doherty
Penelope Lively

Geraldine McCaughrean
Miriam Pressler
Jill Paton Walsh
Jane Yolen

The Girls in the Velvet Frame
Pictures of the Night
Silent snow, Secret Snow
The Tower Room

Alan Gibbons

Computers   Fantasy   Social issues   Sport

8-11

K A Applegate
Neil Arksey
Bernard Ashley
Gillian Cross
Narinder Dhami

Alan Durant
Anthony Horowitz
Robert Leeson
Celia Rees
Benjamin Zephaniah

The Edge
Ganging Up
Julie and Me ... and Michael Owen Makes Three
Julie and Me: Treble Trouble
Street of Tall People
Legendeer Trilogy
Total Football Series

12-14

Morris Gleitzman

Family   Humour   Social issues

8-11

Judy Blume
Elaine Forrestal
Carol Hedges
Anthony Horowitz
Paul Jennings

Louis Sachar
Moya Simons
Sonya Sones
Jerry Spinelli
Sue Townsend

Adults Only
Deadly
Gift of the Gab
Misery Guts
The Other Facts of Life
Two Weeks with the Queen

Sandra Glover

Computers   Ghost/supernatural   Social issues

David Almond
Rachel Anderson

Berlie Doherty
Jacqueline Wilson

Breaking the Rules
Crazy Games
Face to Face
The Girl Who Knew
Nowhere Boy

John Gordon

Fantasy   Ghost/supernatural   Horror

Vivien Alcock
Alan Garner
Ann Halam

Pat Moon
Hugh Scott

The Burning Baby and Other Ghosts
The Giant Under the Snow
Gilray's Ghost
Midwinter Watch
Ordinary Seaman: a Teenage Memoir

Keith Gray

Social issues

Melvin Burgess
Pete Johnson

Robert Swindells

£10,000
Creepers
Dead Trouble
The Runner
Warehouse

Rosa Guy

Family   Social issues

Judy Allen
Nina Bawden
Virginia Hamilton

Julie Johnston
Walter Dean Myers

The Disappearance
The Friends

Margaret Haddix

Science fiction   Thrillers

Julie Bertagna
Louise Cooper
Lois Duncan
Catherine Fisher

Ann Halam
Lesley Howarth
Louise Lawrence

Amongst the Betrayed
Amongst the Hidden
Amongst the Imposters
Running Out of Time
Turnabout

12-14

Ann Halam
Ghost/supernatural   Horror

Joan Aiken
Vivien Alcock
Rachel Anderson
Lois Duncan
John Gordon

Margaret Haddix
Margaret Mahy
Pat Moon
Celia Rees
Hugh Scott

Crying in the Dark
Dr Franklin's Island
The Fear Man
The Powerhouse

12-14

Virginia Hamilton
Family   Fantasy   Other cultures   Other lands

Kate Elizabeth Ernest
Rosa Guy

Julius Lester
Jacqueline Roy

The Magical Adventures of Pretty Pearl
The Planet of Junior Brown
Zeely
Justice Trilogy

Dennis Hamley
Detective mysteries   Historical

5-7 8-11

David Belbin
Henrietta Branford
Karen Cushman

Malachy Doyle
Geraldine McCaughrean

Dead Ringer
The Joslin de Lay Mysteries Series

Ruth Elwin Harris
Family   Romance   War 1914-18

Nina Bawden
Michelle Magorian

Kit Pearson
K M Peyton

Sisters of the Quantock Hills Quartet

Don't forget: Picture Books ∗ Genres ∗ Series ∗ Book Prizes ∗ Bibliography ☞

Carol Hedges
Social issues   Thrillers

Sharon Creech
Anne Fine

Morris Gleitzman
Mary Hooper

Bright Angel
Jigsaw
Red Velvet

Diana Hendry
Family   Fantasy

8-11

Stephen Elboz
William Nicholson

J K Rowling
Hilary McKay

Double Vision
You Can't Kiss It Better
Minders

Harvey Angell Series

12-14

Frances Mary Hendry
Diaries   Historical   Other cultures

Rachel Anderson
Anita Desai
Deborah Ellis

Jamila Gavin
Elizabeth Laird
Bali Rai

The '45 Rising: the Diary of Euphemia Grant
Atlantis
Atlantis in Peril
Chains
Chandra
The Crystal Palace

Quest for a Queen Trilogy

Gaye Hiçyilmaz
Family   Other cultures   Social issues

Deborah Ellis
Nancy Farmer
Elizabeth Laird
Joan Lingard

Beverley Naidoo
Suzanne Fisher Staples
Benjamin Zephaniah

Against the Storm
Coming Home
The Frozen Waterfall
Girl in Red
Watching the Watcher

Nigel Hinton
Adventure   Family   Fantasy   Thrillers

8-11

Yinka Adebayo
S E Hinton
Pete Johnson

Louis Sachar
John Rowe Townsend

Collision Course
Out of the Darkness
The Buddy Series

S E Hinton
Social issues

12-14

Yinka Adebayo
Melvin Burgess
Nigel Hinton

Pete Johnson
Catherine MacPhail

The Outsiders
Rumblefish
Taming the Star Runner

Elizabeth Honey
Computers   Humour

Ros Asquith
Steve Barlow and Steve
   Skidmore

Narinder Dhami
Rosie Rushton
Moya Simons

45 and 47 Stella Street and Everything That Happened
Remote Man
What Do You Think, Feezal?

Mary Hooper
Family   Letters   Romance   Social issues

5-7 8-11

Yvonne Coppard
Chris d'Lacey
Paula Danziger
Carol Hedges
Cathy Hopkins

Millie Murray
Dyan Sheldon
Martin Waddell
Virginia Euwer Wolff

The Boyfriend Trap
Holly
Letters to Liz Series
The Megan Series

Cathy Hopkins
Family   Humour   Romance   Social issues

Mary Hooper
Louise Rennison

Dyan Sheldon

Mates, Dates and Inflatable Bras
Mates, Dates and Portobello Princesses
White Lies and Barefaced Truths

Anthony Horowitz
Adventure   Horror   Humour   Thrillers

8-11

Vivien Alcock
David Belbin
Eoin Colfer
Alan Gibbons
Morris Gleitzman

Eva Ibbotson
Robert Leeson
Anthony Masters
Gary Paulsen
Philip Ridley

Horowitz Horror: Nine Nasty Stories to Chill You to the Bone
Point Blanc
Skeleton Key
South by South East
Stormbreaker

Lesley Howarth
Environment   Family   Science fiction   Thrillers

8-11

Julie Bertagna
Louise Cooper
William Corlett
Annie Dalton
Margaret Haddix

Rhiannon Lassiter
Jan Mark
William Nicholson
Celia Rees
Gillian Rubinstein

Carwash
The Flower King
Maphead
Maphead 2
Quirx
Ultraviolet
Weather Eye

12-14

Janni Howker Social issues

Henrietta Branford
Melvin Burgess

Jan Mark
Robert Swindells

Badger on the Barge
Isaac Campion
The Nature of the Beast

Eva Ibbotson   Adventure   Ghost/supernatural   Humour

8-11

Gillian Cross
Jean Craighead George

Anthony Horowitz

Journey to the River Sea
Which Witch

Brian Jacques   Adventure   Fantasy

8-11

William Corlett
Robin Jarvis
Stephen Moore

Terry Pratchett
Kate Thompson
J R R Tolkien

Castaways of the Flying Dutchman
Redwall Series

Robin Jarvis   Fantasy

8-11

Joan Aiken
Susan Cooper
William Corlett
Catherine Fisher

Brian Jacques
Diana Wynne Jones
Stephen Moore
Terry Pratchett

The Deptford Histories Series
Intrigues of the Reflected Realm Series
Tales for the Wyrd Museum Series
The Whitby Witches Series

Don't forget: Picture Books * Genres * Series * Book Prizes * Bibliography ☞

12-14

Paul Jennings

Ghost/supernatural   Humour   Thrillers

8-11

Alan Durant
Morris Gleitzman
Stephen Moore

Philip Ridley
Moya Simons

Eye of Evil
Sucked In: the Story of an Appendix on the Loose
Tongue-tied
Unmentionable!
Unreal!
Unseen

12-14

Angela Johnson

Social issues

Melvin Burgess
Julie Johnston

Elizabeth Laird

Humming Whispers
Songs of Faith
Toning the Sweep

Catherine R Johnson

Historical   Social issues

Karen Cushman
Leon Garfield
Millie Murray

Ruth Park
Miriam Pressler
Jacqueline Roy

In Black and White
Hero
Stella

Pete Johnson

Fantasy   Ghost/supernatural   Social issues

8-11

Veronica Bennett
Malorie Blackman
Alan Durant
Keith Gray
Nigel Hinton

S E Hinton
Robert Leeson
Jan Mark
Louis Sachar

Eyes of the Alien
Headless Ghost
Rescuing Dad
Runaway Teacher
The Vision

Friends Forever Series

Julie Johnston Social issues

Bernard Ashley
Anne Fine
Paula Fox

Rosa Guy
Angela Johnson
Jacqueline Roy

Adam and Eve and Pinch Me
Hero of Lesser Causes

Diana Wynne Jones Fantasy

8-11

12-14

Joan Aiken
Stephen Elboz
Catherine Fisher
Alan Garner
Robin Jarvis

Ursula Le Guin
Jenny Nimmo
Philip Pullman
J K Rowling
Laura C Stevenson

Fire and Hemlock
Hexwood
Power of Three
Worlds of Chrestomanci Series

Brian Keaney Family Social issues Thrillers

Veronica Bennett
Tim Bowler
Gillian Cross
Berlie Doherty

Linda Newberry
Sonya Sones
Cynthia Voigt

Balloon House
Bitter Fruit
Falling for Joshua
Family Secrets
Private Life of Georgia Brown

Christa Laird War 1939-45

Rachel Anderson
Elizabeth Lutzeier

Michael Morpurgo
Robert Westall

Beyond the Wall
But Can the Phoenix Sing?
Shadow of the Wall

Elizabeth Laird
Adventure Family Other cultures Social issues

8-11

Henrietta Branford
Gillian Cross
Farrukh Dhondy
Deborah Ellis
Frances Mary Hendry

Gaye Hiçyilmaz
Angela Johnson
Joan Lingard
Beverley Naidoo
Jill Paton Walsh

Forbidden Ground
Jake's Tower
Jay
Kiss the Dust
Red Sky in the Morning

12-14

Rhiannon Lassiter
Computers Fantasy Science fiction

K A Applegate
Lesley Howarth
Lois Lowry

Tamora Pierce
Chloë Rayban
Gillian Rubinstein

Hex Series

Louise Lawrence
Fantasy Science fiction

K A Applegate
Louise Cooper
Catherine Fisher
Margaret Haddix

Robert C O'Brien
Tamora Pierce
Susan Price
Gillian Rubinstein

Children of the Dust
Crowlings
Dreamweaver
Shadow of Mordican

Ursula Le Guin
Fantasy Magic

Susan Cooper
Stephen Elboz
Catherine Fisher
Jostein Gaarder

Diana Wynne Jones
Tamora Pierce
Philip Pullman
J R R Tolkien

The Farthest Shore
The Other Wind
Tehuna
The Tombs of Atuan
A Wizard of Earthsea

Robert Leeson

Family   Letters   Mythology   Social issues

Bernard Ashley
Veronica Bennett
Kevin Crossley-Holland
Berlie Doherty
Anne Fine

Alan Gibbons
Anthony Horowitz
Pete Johnson
Michael Morpurgo
Martin Waddell

Liar
Red, White & Blue
The Song of Arthur

Julius Lester

Historical   Other cultures   Other lands

Virginia Hamilton
Gary Paulsen

Mildred D Taylor
James Watson

Long Journey Home
Two Love Stories

12-14

Joan Lingard

Social issues   War

5-7

Lynne Reid Banks
Gaye Hiçyilmaz
Elizabeth Laird
Elizabeth Lutzeier
Bel Mooney

Linda Newberry
Martin Waddell
James Watson
Benjamin Zephaniah

Dark Shadows
Lizzie's Leaving
Me and My Shadow
Natasha's Will

Kevin and Sadie Series
Maggie Series

Penelope Lively

Ghost/supernatural   Historical

5-7 8-11

Joan Aiken
Nina Bawden

Gary Blackwood
Adèle Geras

The Driftway
The Ghost of Thomas Kempe
The House in Norham Gardens

Errol Lloyd

Family

Kate Elizabeth Ernest
Millie Murray
James Watson

In a Strange Land
Many Rivers to Cross

Lois Lowry

Fantasy War 1939-45

8-11

Marita Conlon-McKenna
Louise Cooper
Rhiannon Lassiter
William Nicholson
Tamora Pierce
Sue Welford

Gathering Blue
The Giver
Number the Stars

Elizabeth Lutzeier

Other cultures Social issues War 1939-45

Marita Conlon-McKenna
Christa Laird
Joan Lingard
Michael Morpurgo
Bali Rai
James Watson

Bound for America
The Coldest Winter
Lost for Words
The Wall

Geraldine McCaughrean

Family Fantasy Hist'l Other cultures

5-7 8-11

Henrietta Branford
Gillian Cross
Peter Dickinson
Berlie Doherty
Malachy Doyle
Adèle Geras
Dennis Hamley
Sally Prue
Jill Paton Walsh

Forever X
Kite Rider
A Pilgrim's Progress
Plundering Paradise
The Stones are Hatching
Stop the Train

Hilary McKay

Family   Humour   Social issues
5-7 8-11

Berlie Doherty
Diana Hendry

Rosie Rushton

Saffy's Angel
The Exiles

Catherine MacPhail

Fantasy   Social issues
8-11

Bernard Ashley
Julie Bertagna
Melvin Burgess

S E Hinton
Robert Swindells

Bad Company
A Kind of Magic
Run, Zan, Run
Tribes

Michelle Magorian

Family   War 1939-45
8-11

Rachel Anderson
Nina Bawden
Theresa Breslin
Marita Conlon-McKenna
Sharon Creech

Ruth Elwin Harris
Kit Pearson
K M Peyton
James Riordan
John Rowe Townsend

Cuckoo in the Nest
Goodnight Mister Tom
A Little Love Song
A Spoonful of Jam

Margaret Mahy

Fantasy   Ghost/supernatural
5-7 8-11

Lois Duncan
Susan Gates
Ann Halam

Pat Moon
Bel Mooney

The Changeover
The Haunting
Memory
The Tricksters

12-14

Jan Mark

Family Fantasy Social issues

5-7 8-11

Bernard Ashley
Gillian Cross
Lesley Howarth
Janni Howker

Pete Johnson
Pat Moon
William Nicholson
Sally Prue

Eclipse of the Century
The Lady with Iron Bones
They Do Things Differently There

12-14

Anthony Masters

Diaries Ghost/supernat Horror Thrillers

5-7 8-11

Annie Dalton
Peter Dickinson
Alan Durant
Susan Gates
Anthony Horowitz

Malcolm Rose
Hugh Scott
Darren Shan
R L Stine
Robert Westall

The Drop
Finding Joe
Fire Starter
Lights Out
Wicked

Dark Diaries Series

Sue Mayfield

Social issues

Millie Murray
Bette Paul
Dyan Sheldon
Sonya Sones

Cynthia Voigt
Martin Waddell
Sue Welford
Virginia Euwer Wolff

Blue
Reckless
A Time to be Born

Don't forget: Picture Books ∗ Genres ∗ Series ∗ Book Prizes ∗ Bibliography ☞

Pat Moon
Ghost/supernatural   Social issues

David Almond
Robert Cormier
Berlie Doherty
John Gordon
Ann Halam

Margaret Mahy
Jan Mark
Bette Paul
Celia Rees
Sonya Sones

Double Image
Ghost of Sadie Kimber
Nathan's Switch
The Spying Game

Bel Mooney
Historical   Romance   Social issues

5-7

Lynne Reid Banks
Joan Lingard

Margaret Mahy
Miriam Pressler

A Flower of Jet

Stephen Moore
Fantasy

Stephen Elboz
Brian Jacques
Robin Jarvis

Paul Jennings
Terry Pratchett

Dead Edward
Skin and Bone
Tooth and Claw

Michael Morpurgo
Historical   School   Social issues   War 1939-45

5-7 8-11

Rachel Anderson
Martin Booth
Marita Conlon-McKenna
Kevin Crossley-Holland
Jean Craighead George

Christa Laird
Robert Leeson
Elizabeth Lutzeier
James Riordan
Robert Westall

The Ghost of Grania O'Malley
Out of the Ashes
The Sleeping Sword
Waiting for Anya
War Horse
The War of Jenkins' Ear

12-14

Millie Murray
Family   Other cultures   Social issues

Mary Hooper
Catherine R Johnson
Errol Lloyd

Sue Mayfield
Jacqueline Roy

Jade
Kiesha
Lady A, a Teenage DJ
Sorrelle

Walter Dean Myers
Social issues

Yinka Adebayo
Malorie Blackman

Rosa Guy

Darnell Rock Reporting
Scorpions
Somewhere in the Darkness

Beverley Naidoo
Other lands   Social issues

Lynne Reid Banks
James Berry
Deborah Ellis
Kate Elizabeth Ernest
Nancy Farmer

Gaye Hiçyilmaz
Elizabeth Laird
Robert Swindells
James Watson
Benjamin Zephaniah

Journey to Jo'burg
No Turning Back
The Other Side of Truth
Out of Bounds

Linda Newberry
Family   War 1939-45

Martin Booth
Tim Bowler
Theresa Breslin
Brian Keaney

Joan Lingard
Jill Paton Walsh
Robert Westall

Blitz Boys
Breaktime
The Damage Done
No Way Back
Windfall
Shouting Wind Trilogy

William Nicholson

8-11

K A Applegate
Peter Dickinson
Diana Hendry
Lesley Howarth
Lois Lowry

Jan Mark
Susan Price
Philip Pullman
J K Rowling

Firesong
Slaves of the Mastery
The Wind Singer

Jenny Nimmo

Family   Fantasy   Ghost/supernatural

5-7 8-11

Terence Blacker
Diana Wynne Jones
Tamora Pierce

Stephen Potts
J K Rowling

Griffin's Castle
Milo's Wolves
The Rinaldi Ring

Robert C O'Brien

Science fiction   War

8-11

Louise Lawrence

Robert Swindells

Z for Zachariah

Ruth Park

Environment   Historical: Victorian

Catherine R Johnson

Katherine Paterson

My Sister Sif
Playing Beatie Bow

Katherine Paterson

Family   Historical

8-11

Natalie Babbitt
Tim Bowler
Sharon Creech

Gillian Cross
Ruth Park
Cynthia Voigt

Bridge to Terabithia
Come Sing Jimmy Jo
Jacob Have I Loved
Preacher's Boy

12-14

141

Bette Paul

12-14

Family

Sue Mayfield
Pat Moon

Mildred D Taylor
Cynthia Voigt

Becca's Race
Ladlass
Variations on a Dream

Gary Paulsen

Adventure   Family   Historical   War

8-11

David Belbin
Melvin Burgess
Peter Dickinson
Anthony Horowitz

Julius Lester
Louis Sachar
Mildred D Taylor
Jill Paton Walsh

The Car
Mr Tucket
Nightjohn
Sarny
Tucket's Ride
White Fox
The Hatchett Series

Kit Pearson

War 1939-45

Theresa Breslin
Marita Conlon-McKenna

Ruth Elwin Harris
Michelle Magorian

War Guests Trilogy

K M Peyton

Pony/horse   Romance   Thrillers   War 1914-18

5-7 8-11

Nina Bawden
Ruth Elwin Harris

Michelle Magorian
John Rowe Townsend

Blind Beauty
A Midsummer Night's Death
Prove Yourself a Hero
Flambards Series

Helena Pielichaty

Family   Social issues

8-11

Malorie Blackman
Judy Blume
Josephine Feeney

Anne Fine
Jack Gantos
Jacqueline Wilson

Getting Rid of Karenna
Jade's Story
Never Ever

Tamora Pierce

Fantasy   Magic

12-14

Susan Cooper
Stephen Elboz
Rhiannon Lassiter
Louise Lawrence
Ursula Le Guin

Lois Lowry
Jenny Nimmo
Susan Price
Katherine Roberts

Circle of Magic Quartet
The Circle Opens Quartet
The Immortals Series
Protector of the Small Series
Song of the Lioness Series

Stephen Potts

Adventure   Historical

8-11

Susan Gates
Jenny Nimmo

Robert Westall

Compass Murphy
Hunting Gumnor
Tommy Trouble

Terry Pratchett

Fantasy   Humour

8-11

Eoin Colfer
Brian Jacques
Robin Jarvis

Stephen Moore
Lemony Snicket
Laura C Stevenson

The Amazing Maurice and his Educated Rodents
Johnny and the Bomb
Johnny and the Dead
Only You Can Save Mankind
Truckers

The Discworld Series

Miriam Pressler
Historical   Other cultures   Social issues

Rachel Anderson
Gary Blackwood
Jamila Gavin

Adèle Geras
Catherine R Johnson
Bel Mooney

Shylock's Daughter
Malka

Susan Price
Fantasy   Ghost/supernatural   Science fiction

8-11

David Almond
Karen Cushman
Alan Garner
Louise Lawrence

William Nicholson
Tamora Pierce
Sally Prue
Celia Rees

The Bearwood Witch
The Bone Dog
The Ghost Drum
The Sterkarm Handshake
The Story Collector

Alison Prince
Family   Historical

5-7 8-11

Rachel Anderson
Leon Garfield
Jamila Gavin

Rosemary Sutcliff
Mildred D Taylor

Bird Boy
The Fortune Teller
Here Comes a Candle
Oranges and Murder
Turnaround

Sally Prue
Fantasy   Social issues

Peter Dickinson
Alan Garner
Geraldine McCaughrean

Jan Mark
Susan Price

Cold Tom

Philip Pullman
Fantasy   Historical: Vict   Social issues   Thrillers

8-11

Natalie Babbitt
Annie Dalton
Peter Dickinson
Alan Garner
Diana Wynne Jones

Ursula Le Guin
William Nicholson
J K Rowling
Kate Thompson
J R R Tolkien

The Broken Bridge
The Ruby in the Smoke
The Shadow in the North
The Tiger in the Well
The Tin Princess
White Mercedes

His Dark Materials Trilogy

Bali Rai
Other cultures

Narinder Dhami
Jamila Gavin

Frances Mary Hendry
Elizabeth Lutzeier

Dream On
(Un)arranged Marriage

Chloë Rayban
Computers   Romance   Science fiction

K A Applegate
Ros Asquith
Malorie Blackman

Rhiannon Lassiter
Rosie Rushton

Love in Cyberia
Terminal Chic
Virtual Sexual Reality
Wild Child

12-14

on't forget: Picture Books * Genres * Series * Book Prizes * Bibliography ☞

45

Celia Rees Ghost/supernatural   Historical   Social issues   Thrillers

8-11

David Belbin
Julie Bertagna
Malorie Blackman
Alan Gibbons
Ann Halam

Lesley Howarth
Pat Moon
Susan Price
Marcus Sedgwick

The Bailey Game
City of Shadows
The Host Rides Out
The Sorceress
Truth or Dare
Witch Child

12-14

Louise Rennison Diaries   Humour   Romance

Ros Asquith
Steve Barlow and
   Steve Skidmore
Yvonne Coppard
Josephine Feeney

Cathy Hopkins
Rosie Rushton
Dyan Sheldon
Sue Townsend

Angus, Thongs and Full Frontal Snogging
Dancing in my Nuddy-Pants
It's OK, I'm Wearing Really Big Knickers!
Knocked Out By My Nunga-Nungas

Philip Ridley Fantasy   Humour   Social issues

8-11

Eoin Colfer
Anthony Horowitz

Paul Jennings

Dakota of the White Flats
Mercedes Ice
Scribbleboy

Don't forget: Picture Books * Genres * Series * Book Prizes * Bibliography ☞

James Riordan

Martin Booth
Robert Cormier
Michelle Magorian
Michael Morpurgo

Stewart Ross
James Watson
Robert Westall
Jane Yolen

The Enemy: a Story of World War II
Match of Death
The Prisoner
Sweet Clarinet
When Guns Fall Silent

Katherine Roberts
Fantasy   Mythology

Susan Cooper
Tamora Pierce

J R R Tolkien

The Babylon Game
Crystal Mask
The Great Pyramid Robbery
Song Quest
Spellfall

Malcolm Rose
Social issues   Thrillers

Bernard Ashley
David Belbin
Robert Cormier

Anthony Masters
Robert Swindells
Jane Yolen

Clone
Flying Blind
Plague

Stewart Ross
Other cultures   War

Rachel Anderson

James Riordan

False Papers: a Story from World War I
Only a Matter of Time: a Story from Kosovo
The Star Houses: a Story from the Holocaust

J K Rowling

8-11

Fantasy   Magic   School

Eoin Colfer
William Corlett
Stephen Elboz
Diana Hendry
Diana Wynne Jones

William Nicholson
Jenny Nimmo
Philip Pullman
Laura C Stevenson

Harry Potter Series

12-14

Jacqueline Roy

Family   Social issues

Malorie Blackman
Virginia Hamilton
Catherine R Johnson

Julie Johnston
Millie Murray

A Daughter Like Me
Fat Chance
Playing It Cool

Gillian Rubinstein

Science fiction

K A Applegate
Lesley Howarth

Rhiannon Lassiter
Louise Lawrence

Beyond the Labyrinth
Foxspell

The Space Demons Trilogy

Rosie Rushton

Humour   Letters   Romance   Social issues

Judy Blume
Yvonne Coppard
Paula Danziger
Josephine Feeney
Elizabeth Honey

Hilary McKay
Chloë Rayban
Louise Rennison
Dyan Sheldon
Jacqueline Wilson

Break Point
How Could You Do This To Me, Mum?
Jessica
Just Don't Make a Scene, Mum!
Melissa
Tell Me I'm OK Really

Louis Sachar
Humour   School   Social issues

David Almond
Elaine Forrestal
Jack Gantos
Morris Gleitzman
Nigel Hinton

Pete Johnson
Gary Paulsen
Nicky Singer
Lemony Snicket
Jerry Spinelli

The Boy Who Lost His Face
Dogs Don't Tell Jokes
Holes
Someday Angeline
There's a Boy in the Girls' Bathroom

12-14

Hugh Scott
Ghost/supernatural   Horror

Joan Aiken
Vivien Alcock
Lois Duncan
Leon Garfield

John Gordon
Ann Halam
Anthony Masters
Marcus Sedgwick

A Box of Tricks
Camera Obscura
The Gargoyle
The Ghosts of Ravens Crag
A Ghost Waiting
The Haunted Sand

Marcus Sedgwick   Environment   Ghost/supernatural   Historical

Judy Allen
David Almond
Karen Cushman

Celia Rees
Hugh Scott

The Dark Horse
Floodland
Witch Hill

Darren Shan
Horror

Anthony Masters

R L Stine

The Saga of Darren Shan

Dyan Sheldon

Romance   Social issues

5-7 8-11

Mary Hooper
Cathy Hopkins
Sue Mayfield
Louise Rennison

Rosie Rushton
Sue Welford
Virginia Euwer Wolff

And Baby Makes Two
Confessions of a Teenage Drama Queen
Tall, Thin and Blonde

Moya Simons

Family   Humour

Ros Asquith
Yvonne Coppard
Morris Gleitzman

Elizabeth Honey
Paul Jennings

Dead Funny
Hatty's Hotline
Sit Down Mum, There's Something I've Got to Tell You

Nicky Singer

Detective mysteries   Social issues

Sharon Creech
Elaine Forrestal

Louis Sachar
Jerry Spinelli

Feather Boy

Lemony Snicket

Fantasy   Humour

8-11

Vivien Alcock
Eoin Colfer

Terry Pratchett
Louis Sachar

A Series of Unfortunate Events Series

Sonya Sones

Family   Social issues

David Almond
Sharon Creech
Helen Dunmore
Morris Gleitzman
Brian Keaney

Sue Mayfield
Pat Moon
Jerry Spinelli
Jacqueline Wilson
Virginia Euwer Wolff

Stop Pretending; What Happened When My Sister Went Crazy
What My Mother Doesn't Know

Jerry Spinelli Romance   School   Social issues

Sharon Creech
Morris Gleitzman
Louis Sachar

Nicky Singer
Sonya Sones
Virginia Euwer Wolff

The Mighty Crashman (previously published as *Crash*)
Stargirl
Wringer

Suzanne Fisher Staples   Other cultures   Other lands

12-14

Anita Desai
Deborah Ellis

Jamila Gavin
Gaye Hiçyilmaz

Daughter of the Wind
Shiva's Fire
Storm

Laura C Stevenson   Fantasy

Diana Wynne Jones
Terry Pratchett

J K Rowling

All the King's Horses

R L Stine   Horror

8-11

Anthony Masters

Darren Shan

Goosebumps Series

Rosemary Sutcliff   Historical

8-11

Henrietta Branford
Susan Cooper
Kevin Crossley-Holland

Leon Garfield
Alison Prince

King Arthur Stories
Outcast
Song for a Dark Queen
The Eagle of the Ninth Sequence

Robert Swindells
Science fiction   Social issues   Thrillers   War

5-7 8-11

Martin Booth
Keith Gray
Janni Howker
Catherine MacPhail
Beverley Naidoo

Robert C O'Brien
Malcolm Rose
Kate Thompson
Benjamin Zephaniah

Abomination
Brother in the Land
Dosh
Smash!
Stone Cold
Wrecked

12-14

Mildred D Taylor
Historical   Other lands

Jamila Gavin
Julius Lester
Bette Paul

Gary Paulsen
Alison Prince

Let the Circle be Unbroken
Road to Memphis
Roll of Thunder, Hear My Cry

Kate Thompson
Fantasy   Science fiction

8-11

K A Applegate
William Corlett
Peter Dickinson

Brian Jacques
Philip Pullman
Robert Swindells

The Alchemist's Apprentice
The Beguilers
The Missing Link
Only Human
Switchers Trilogy

J R R Tolkien
Fantasy

8-11

Susan Cooper
Stephen Elboz
Brian Jacques

Ursula Le Guin
Philip Pullman
Katherine Roberts

Farmer Giles of Ham
The Lord of the Rings

Theresa Tomlinson — Family Historical

5-7 8-11

Henrietta Branford
Karen Cushman

Jill Paton Walsh

The Flither Pickers
The Path of the She-Wolf
The Rope Carrier
Riding the Waves

John Rowe Townsend — Adventure Thrillers

Nigel Hinton
Michelle Magorian

K M Peyton

Gumble's Yard
The Intruder
The Islanders

Sue Townsend — Diaries Humour

Steve Barlow and
  Steve Skidmore
Morris Gleitzman

Louise Rennison
Jacqueline Wilson

Adrian Mole Series

Jean Ure — Family Other cultures Romance Social issues

5-7 8-11

Ros Asquith
Gillian Cross

Martin Waddell

Family Fan Club
Get a Life!
Love is Forever
A Twist in Time

Cynthia Voigt — Family Other cultures Other lands Social issues

Paula Fox
Brian Keaney
Sue Mayfield

Katherine Paterson
Bette Paul
Martin Waddell

Bad, Badder, Baddest
Born to be Bad
Tillerman Series

12-14

153

Martin Waddell
Family   Social issues   War

also writes as Catherine Sefton   5-7 8-11

Berlie Doherty   Sue Mayfield
Mary Hooper   Jean Ure
Robert Leeson   Cynthia Voigt
Joan Lingard

The Beat of the Drum
The Kidnapping of Suzie Q
The Life and Loves of Zoe T Curley
Starry Night
Tango's Baby

12-14

Jill Paton Walsh
Historical   War 1939-45

5-7

Henrietta Branford   Geraldine McCaughrean
Theresa Breslin   Linda Newberry
Leon Garfield   Gary Paulsen
Adèle Geras   Theresa Tomlinson
Elizabeth Laird

Fireweed
Grace
Parcel of Patterns

James Watson
Other cultures   Social issues   Thrillers

Lynne Reid Banks   Errol Lloyd
James Berry   Elizabeth Lutzeier
Robert Cormier   Beverley Naidoo
Julius Lester   James Riordan
Joan Lingard

The Freedom Tree
Justice of the Dagger
Talking in Whispers
Ticket to Prague

Sylvia Waugh
Family   Fantasy

8-11

Natalie Babbitt   Lynne Reid Banks

The Mennyms Series

Sue Welford

Helen Dunmore
Alan Durant
Lois Lowry

Sue Mayfield
Dyan Sheldon

The Night After Tomorrow
Out of the Blue
The Shadow of August

Robert Westall
Adventure Ghost/supernat Sci fiction War '39-45

8-11

12-14

Martin Booth
Peter Dickinson
Christa Laird
Anthony Masters

Michael Morpurgo
Linda Newberry
Stephen Potts
James Riordan

Gulf
The Promise
The Stones of Muncaster Cathedral
Urn Burial
The Watch House
The Wind Eye

Jacqueline Wilson
Diaries Family Humour Romance Social issues

5-7 8-11

Judy Blume
Yvonne Coppard
Paula Danziger
Narinder Dhami
Anne Fine

Sandra Glover
Helena Pielichaty
Rosie Rushton
Sonya Sones
Sue Townsend

The Dare Game
Dustbin Baby
Girls Out Late
The Illustrated Mum
Lola Rose
Secrets

Don't forget: Picture Books * Genres * Series * Book Prizes * Bibliography ☞

Virginia Euwer Wolff   Other lands   Romance   Social issues

Mary Hooper   Sonya Sones
Sue Mayfield   Jerry Spinelli
Dyan Sheldon

Make Lemonade
True Believer

Jane Yolen   War 1939-45

Adèle Geras   Malcolm Rose
James Riordan

The Devil's Arithmetic

Benjamin Zephaniah   Other cultures   Social issues   War

Robert Cormier   Joan Lingard
Farrukh Dhondy   Beverley Naidoo
Alan Gibbons   Robert Swindells
Gaye Hiçyilmaz

Face
Refugee Boy

Don't forget: Picture Books * Genres * Series * Book Prizes * Bibliography ☞

12-14

Picture Books for Older Readers

There is no universal definition of what constitutes a 'picture book for older readers'. The following eclectic collection is compiled from suggestions from *Who Next?* advisors across the UK; the final selection is mine. Lesley Cooper and I decided to include this section in *Who Next?* because we recognised that picture books for older readers contribute so much to the development and enjoyment of reading. Most books are multi-layered and older children have much to gain from them. They can be used to:

- provide fun and enjoyment
- widen horizons
- challenge perceptions
- stimulate imagination
- provide ideas for new ways of seeing
- investigate how pictures and words complement and extend each other.

Picture books for older readers are listed alphabetically by author and/or illustrator ✐. Themes are included only for very general guidance; like most good books they defy categorisation. These books are listed separately from the main sequence because the importance here is on the illustration and the story equally and this does not lend itself to *Who Next?* like comparisons.

I hope that by including this selection, we are providing even more ideas for *Who Next?*

Allan Ahlberg   ✐ Janet Ahlberg

It Was a Dark and Stormy Night	Adventure

Victor Ambrus ✐

Dracula	Horror
Son of Dracula	Horror
Dracula's Bedtime Storybook	Horror

Jeannie Baker ✐

The Hidden Forest	Environment
Window	Environment
Where the Forest Meets the Sea	Environment, Other lands
Home in the Sky	Other lands

Istvan Banyai ✐

Zoom	Perception
ReZoom	Perception

Antonia Barber   ✐ Nicola Bayley

The Mousehole Cat	Traditional

Graeme Base ✎

Animalia	Perception
The Water Hole	Environment

Quentin Blake ✎

The Green Ship	Fantasy & Adventure
Clown	Fantasy & Adventure
Zagazoo	Family
A Sailing Boat in the Sky	Environment

Becky Bloom ✎ Pascal Biet

A Cultivated Wolf	Humour

Louise Borden ✎ Michael Foreman

The Little Ships	War (WWII)

Herbie Brennan ✎ Cathy Gale

Frankenstella and the Video Shop Monster!	Humour, Social issues

Raymond Briggs ✎

Fungus the Bogeyman	Humour
When the Wind Blows	War (Nuclear)
The Bear	Fantasy
Father Christmas	Humour
Ethel & Ernest	Family
The Man	Social issues
Ug	Historical
Ivor the Invisible	Humour

Anthony Browne ✎

My Dad	Humour, Social issues
Zoo	Humour, Social issues
Willy the Champ	Humour, Social issues
Willy the Dreamer	Humour, Social issues, Art
Willy the Wimp	Humour
The Tunnel	Social issues, Family
Changes	Social issues, Family
A Walk in the Park	Humour, Social issues
Voices in the Park	Humour, Social issues
Gorilla	Humour, Social issues
King Kong	Humour
Piggy Book	Social issues, Family

Eve Bunting ✎ David Wiesner

Night of the Gargoyles	Fantasy

Melvin Burgess · Ruth Brown

The Birdman	Environment

John Burningham ·

Aldo	Social issues
Granpa	Death, Social issues
Whadayamean	Environment

Charles Causley · Michael Foreman

The Merrymaid of Zennor	Traditional tales

Lauren Child ·

Beware of the Storybook Wolves	Humour (Fairy tales)
Clarice Bean, That's Me	Humour
What Planet Are You From Clarice Bean?	Humour (Environment)

Babette Cole ·

Hair in Funny Places	Humour
Dr Dog	Family, Humour
Princess Smartypants	Alternative (Fairy tales)
Prince Cinders	Alternative (Fairy tales)
Two of Everything	Family, Social issues

Peter Collington ·

A Small Miracle	Christmas
The Coming of Surf Man	Social issues

Gary Crew · Marc McBride

The Kraken	Fantasy

Gary Crew · Mark Wilson

Valley of Bones	Environment

Gary Crew · Shaun Tan

The Viewer	Mystery, Fantasy

Gary Crew · Steven Woolman

The Watertower	Mystery, Fantasy

Kevin Crossley-Holland · Charles Keeping

Beowulf	Traditional tales

Roald Dahl   ✎ Quentin Blake

The Giraffe, the Pelly and Me	Fantasy

Roald Dahl

James and the Giant Peach	Fantasy

Ted Dewan ✎

The Sorcerer's Apprentice	Magic

Dr Suess   ✎ Steve Johnson and Lou Fancher

My Many Colored Days	Social issues

Sara Fanelli ✎

Dear Diary	Humour
Wolf	Humour
It's Dreamtime	Humour
A Dog's Life	Humour

Jan Fearnley ✎

Mr Wolf and the Three Bears	Humour (Traditional tales)

Paul Fleischmann   ✎ Kevin Hawkes

Weslandia	Environment

Michael Foreman ✎

Cat in the Manger	Christmas
War and Peas	War (WWII)
All the King's Horses	Traditional tales
War Boy	War (WWII)
War Game	War (WWII)
After the War Was Over	Postwar
Dinosaurs and All That Rubbish	Environment

Fiona French ✎

Snow White in New York	Humour

Vivian French   ✎ Korky Paul

Aesop's Funky Fables	Fables, Poetry

Saxton Freymann and Joost Elffers ✎

How Are You Peeling?: Foods With Moods	Emotions, food

Leon Garfield    Charles Keeping

The Wedding Ghost   Ghosts

Alistair Graham

Full Moon Soup   Humour
Full Moon Afloat:
   All Aboard for the Craziest Cruise of Your Life!   Humour

James Gurney

Dinotopia   Fantasy

Martin Handford

Where's Wally? Series   Humour

Libby Hathorn   Gregory Rogers

Way Home   Social issues

Amy Hest   P J Lynch

When Jessie Came Across the Sea   Historical

Russell Hoban   Ian Andrew

Jim's Lion   Social issues, Death

Russell Hoban   Quentin Blake

Trouble on Thunder Mountain   Environment

Russell Hoban   Patrick Benson

The Sea-thing Child   Fantasy

Shirley Hughes

Enchantment in the Garden   Fantasy
The Lion and the Unicorn   WWII

Ted Hughes   Jackie Morris

How The Whale Became   Animals

Susan Jeffers

Brother Eagle, Sister Sky   Environment

Nina Laden

Roberto the Insect Architect — Art, Humour

Michael Lawrence — Robert Ingpen

The Poppykettle Papers — Traditional (Adventure)

Annalena McAfee — Anthony Browne

The Visitors Who Came to Stay — Social issues, Family

Ian McEwan — Roberto Innocenti

Rose Blanche — WWII

Clement C Moore — Christian Birmingham

The Night Before Christmas — Christmas

Michael Morpurgo — Michael Foreman

Billy the Kid — WWII

Michael Morpurgo — Christina Balit

Blodin the Beast — Fantasy, Fables

Michael Morpurgo — Christian Birmingham

The Silver Swan — Animals

Christopher Myers

Wings — Social issues
Black Cat — Animals

Alfred Noyes — Charles Keeping

The Highway Man — Horror, Ghosts

Richard Platt — Chris Riddell

Castle Diary — History
Pirate Diary — History

Josephine Poole — Angela Barrett

Snow White — Fantasy, Fairy Stories

Tim Preston   ✐ Simon Bartram

Pumpkin Moon   Fantasy

Philip Pullman   ✐ Ian Beck

Puss in Boots   Fantasy, Fairy Stories

Simon Puttock   ✐ Alison Jay

A Ladder to the Stars   Fantasy

Jon Scieszka   ✐ Lane Smith

Maths Curse	Mathematics
The Stinky Cheese Man and Other Fairly Stupid Tales	Humour
Squids Will Be Squids	Fables
Baloney (Henry P)	Humour
The True Story of The Three Little Pigs	Humour

Jon Scieszka   ✐ Steve Johnson

The Frog Prince Continued   Fairy stories

Maurice Sendak ✐

We Are All in the Dumps With Jack & Guy   Humour

Dyan Sheldon   ✐ Gary Blythe

The Whales' Song   Environment

Mary Shelley   ✐ Chris Mould

Mary Shelley's Frankenstein   Horror

Alan Snow ✐

The Truth About Cats	Humour, Animals
How Dogs Really Work	Humour, Animals

Colin Thompson ✐

Looking for Atlantis	Fantasy
How to Live Forever	Fantasy
The Paradise Garden	Fantasy
Falling Angels	Family, Fantasy & Death
The Last Alchemist	Fantasy

Eugene Trivizas   ✐ Helen Oxenbury

The Three Little Wolves and the Big Bad Pig   Humour

Chris Van Allsburg ✎

The Mysteries of Harris Burdick	Mystery, Fantasy
The Polar Express	Mystery, Fantasy
The Widow's Broom	Mystery, Fantasy
The Sweetest Fig	Animals, Morality

Martin Waddell   ✎ Angela Barrett

The Hidden House	Fantasy

Helen Ward   ✎ Wayne Anderson

The Tin Forest	Environmental

✎ Ulises Wensell   Joan Alavedra

They Followed a Bright Star	Christmas

David Wiesner ✎

Tuesday	Fantasy

Margaret Wild   ✎ Ron Brooks

Fox	Friends

Margaret Wild   ✎ Anne Spudvilas

Jenny Angel	Death

Jeanne Willis   ✎ Tony Ross

The Dr Xargle Books	Humour

Bob Wilson

The Stanley Bagshaw Books	Humour

Susan Wojciechowski   ✎ P J Lynch

The Christmas Miracle of Jonathan Toomey	Christmas, Death

Genres and Themes

Adventure

Genres

5-7

Roy Apps
Phyllis Arkle
Malorie Blackman
Jon Blake
Adrian Boote
Henrietta Branford
Herbie Brennan
Jeff Brown
Lisa Bruce
Damon Burnard
Simon Cheshire
Peter Clover
Gillian Cross
Andrew Donkin
Jonathan Emmett
Sarah Garland
Susan Gates
Mick Gowar

Philippa Gregory
Sally Grindley
Douglas Hill
Mary Hoffman
Mary Hooper
Julia Jarman
Ann Jungman
Robert Leeson
Sam McBratney
Marilyn McLaughlin
Colin McNaughton
Andrew Matthews
Kara May
Michaela Morgan
Hilda Offen
Hiawyn Oram
Daniel Postgate

Chris Powling
Alf Prøysen
Shoo Rayner
Margaret Ryan
Dyan Sheldon
Dee Shulman
Alexander McCall
   Smith
Emily Smith
Jeremy Strong
Jean Ure
Martin Waddell
Karen Wallace
Ian Whybrow
David Henry Wilson
Jacqueline Wilson
Philip Wooderson

8-11

Joan Aiken
Roy Apps
Nina Bawden
Terence Blacker
Malorie Blackman
Enid Blyton
Lucy M Boston
Tony Bradman
Henrietta Branford
Herbie Brennan
Michael Coleman
Susan Cooper
W J Corbett
Helen Cresswell
Gillian Cross
Chris d'Lacey
Colin Dann
Franklin W Dixon
Berlie Doherty
Helen Dunmore
Pauline Fisk
Leon Garfield

Alan Garner
Susan Gates
Elizabeth Hawkins
Nigel Hinton
Odo Hirsch
Michael Hoeye
Anthony Horowitz
Pat Hutchins
Eva Ibbotson
Brian Jacques
Allan Frewin Jones
Carolyn Keene
Fiona Kelly
Garry Kilworth
Clive King
Robin Kingsland
Tessa Krailing
Gail Carson Levine
Astrid Lindgren
Penelope Lively
Margaret Mahy
Ann M Martin

Anthony Masters
Anne Merrick
Michael Morpurgo
William Nicholson
Mary Norton
Gary Paulsen
Philippa Pearce
Stephen Potts
Philip Pullman
Arthur Ransome
Catherine Sefton
Dyan Sheldon
Dodie Smith
Russell Stannard
Robert Swindells
Alan Temperley
J R R Tolkien
Nicholas Warburton
Sylvia Waugh
Robert Westall
Ursula Moray Williams

Adventure (cont)

12-14

Joan Aiken
David Belbin
Gary Blackwood
Susan Cooper
Sharon Creech
Gillian Cross

Peter Dickinson
Jean Craighead George
Nigel Hinton
Anthony Horowitz
Eva Ibbotson
Brian Jacques

Elizabeth Laird
William Nicholson
Gary Paulsen
Stephen Potts
John Rowe Townsend
Robert Westall

Animals

5-7

Allan Ahlberg
Judy Allen
Phyllis Arkle
Brian Ball
Alan Baron
Henrietta Branford
Marc Brown
Lindsay Camp
Anne Cassidy
Harriet Castor
Peter Clover
Helen Cresswell
Chris d'Lacey
Jenny Dale
Lucy Daniels
Penny Dolan
Julia Donaldson
Joyce Dunbar
Vivian French
Jane Gardam

Adèle Geras
Pippa Goodhart
Sally Grindley
Elizabeth Hawkins
Judy Hindley
Mary Hoffman
Rose Impey
Anita Jeram
Dick King-Smith
Tessa Krailing
Arnold Lobel
Geraldine McCaughrean
James Marshall
Andrew and Paula
   Martyr
Anthony Masters
Kara May
Nicola Moon
Michaela Morgan
Michael Morpurgo

Margaret Nash
Jenny Nimmo
Hiawyn Oram
Beatrix Potter
Jillian Powell
Alison Prince
Shoo Rayner
Alison Ritchie
Hilary Robinson
Frank Rodgers
Phyllis Root
Angie Sage
Pat Thomson
Jill Tomlinson
Jean Ure
Alison Uttley
Martin Waddell
Colin West
Ian Whybrow
Selina Young

8-11

Richard Adams
Enid Bagnold
Julie Bertagna
Michael Bond
Kathryn Cave
David Clement-Davies
W J Corbett
Emily Costello
Jenny Dale
Lucy Daniels
Colin Dann

Narinder Dhami
Kate di Camillo
Wendy Douthwaite
Mary Ellis
Kenneth Grahame
Elizabeth Hawkins
Michael Hoeye
Mary Hooper
Brenda Jobling
Garry Kilworth
Dick King-Smith

Tessa Krailing
Elizabeth Laird
Hugh Lofting
A A Milne
Linda Newberry
Jenny Oldfield
Philippa Pearce
Anna Sewell
Dodie Smith
Paul Stewart
E B White
Ursula Moray Williams

Genres

Animals (cont)

12-14
Henrietta Branford

Ballet

5-7
Antonia Barber
Harriet Castor
Adèle Geras
Angela Kanter

8-11
Antonia Barber
Adèle Geras
Mal Lewis Jones
Noel Streatfeild

Computers

8-11
Terence Blacker
Malorie Blackman
Betsy Byars
Michael Coleman
Susan Cooper

Gillian Cross
Terrance Dicks
Helen Dunmore
Alan Gibbons
Anthony Horowitz

Lesley Howarth
Julia Jarman
R L Stine
Jeremy Strong

12-14
Terence Blacker
Malorie Blackman
Paula Danziger

Helen Dunmore
Alan Gibbons
Sandra Glover

Elizabeth Honey
Rhiannon Lassiter
Chloë Rayban

Detective mystery

5-7
Herbie Brennan

8-11
Nina Bawden
Malorie Blackman
Thomas Bloor
Enid Blyton
Franklin W Dixon
Dennis Hamley

Odo Hirsch
Pat Hutchins
Allan Frewin Jones
Carolyn Keene
Fiona Kelly

Robin Kingsland
Catherine MacPhail
Ann M Martin
Magdalen Nabb
Hazel Townson

12-14
Dennis Hamley
Nicky Singer

Diaries

8-11

Sharon Creech
Lucy Daniels
Clive Dickinson

Anne Fine
Helena Pielichaty
Frances Thomas

Jean Ure
Ian Whybrow

12-14

Steve Barlow and
   Steve Skidmore
Yvonne Coppard

Sharon Creech
Frances Mary Hendry
Anthony Masters

Louise Rennison
Sue Townsend
Jacqueline Wilson

Environment

5-7

Jane Gardam

8-11

Richard Adams
Tony Bradman
W J Corbett

Lesley Howarth
Ted Hughes

Clive King
Robert C O'Brien

12-14

Henrietta Branford
Melvin Burgess

Lesley Howarth
Ruth Park

Marcus Sedgwick

Family

5-7

Allan Ahlberg
Rachel Anderson
Elizabeth Arnold
Brian Ball
Claire Bevan
Jon Blake
Theresa Breslin
Joyce Lancaster
   Brisley
Marc Brown
Ann Cameron
Chris d'Lacey
Helen Dunmore
Dorothy Edwards

Anne Fine
Jane Gardam
Sarah Garland
Jamila Gavin
Adèle Geras
Judy Hindley
Mary Hooper
Rose Impey
Julia Jarman
Angela Kanter
Dick King-Smith
Jenny Koralek
Joan Lingard
Penelope Lively

Alan MacDonald
Hilary McKay
Jan Mark
Barbara Mitchelhill
Nicola Moon
Bel Mooney
Michael Morpurgo
Magdalen Nabb
Jenny Nimmo
Hilda Offen
Brian Patten
Ann Pilling
Daniel Postgate
Beatrix Potter

Family (cont)

Family (cont)

5-7 (cont)

Jillian Powell
Chris Powling
Alison Ritchie
Margaret Ryan
Angie Sage

Francesca Simon
Emily Smith
Wendy Smith
Paul Stewart
Jeremy Strong

Pat Thomson
Karen Wallace
Colin West
David Henry Wilson
Jacqueline Wilson

8-11

Allan Ahlberg
Joan Aiken
Vivien Alcock
Louisa May Alcott
David Almond
Rachel Anderson
Bernard Ashley
Lynne Reid Banks
Nina Bawden
Julie Bertagna
Thomas Bloor
Judy Blume
Michael Bond
Lucy M Boston
Frances Hodgson
   Burnett
Betsy Byars
Beverly Cleary
Susan M Coolidge
Sharon Creech
Helen Cresswell
Richmal Crompton
Kevin Crossley-Holland
Chris d'Lacey
Annie Dalton
Paula Danziger
Kate di Camillo

Berlie Doherty
Anne Fine
Jostein Gaarder
Jack Gantos
Susan Gates
Jamila Gavin
Adèle Geras
Morris Gleitzman
Debi Gliori
Rumer Godden
Diana Hendry
Rose Impey
Julia Jarman
Jonathan Kebbe
Dick King-Smith
Robin Klein
Tessa Krailing
Elizabeth Laird
Sheila Lavelle
Lois Lowry
Hilary McKay
Catherine MacPhail
Michelle Magorian
Margaret Mahy
Jan Mark
Ann M Martin
William Mayne

L M Montgomery
E Nesbit
Linda Newberry
Jenny Nimmo
Andrew Norriss
Mary Norton
Katherine Paterson
Philippa Pearce
Helena Pielichaty
Ann Pilling
Alison Prince
Arthur Ransome
Philip Ridley
Francesca Simon
E F Smith
Johanna Spyri
Noel Streatfeild
Jeremy Strong
Ruth Symes
Frances Thomas
Theresa Tomlinson
Hazel Townson
P L Travers
Ann Turnbull
Martin Waddell
Laura Ingalls Wilder
Jacqueline Wilson

12-14

David Almond
Rachel Anderson
Bernard Ashley
Ros Asquith
Natalie Babbitt
Nina Bawden
Malorie Blackman
Judy Blume

Tim Bowler
Theresa Breslin
Yvonne Coppard
Sharon Creech
Narinder Dhami
Berlie Doherty
Helen Dunmore
Kate Elizabeth Ernest

Josephine Feeney
Anne Fine
Elaine Forrestal
Jack Gantos
Adèle Geras
Morris Gleitzman
Rosa Guy
Virginia Hamilton

Genres

169

12-14 (cont)

Ruth Elwin Harris
Diana Hendry
Gaye Hiçyilmaz
Nigel Hinton
Mary Hooper
Cathy Hopkins
Lesley Howarth
Brian Keaney
Elizabeth Laird
Robert Leeson
Errol Lloyd

Geraldine McCaughrean
Hilary McKay
Michelle Magorian
Jan Mark
Millie Murray
Linda Newberry
Jenny Nimmo
Katherine Paterson
Bette Paul
Gary Paulsen
Helena Pielichaty

Alison Prince
Jacqueline Roy
Moya Simons
Sonya Sones
Theresa Tomlinson
Jean Ure
Cynthia Voigt
Martin Waddell
Sylvia Waugh
Jacqueline Wilson

Fantasy

5-7

Adrian Boote
Tony Bradman
Henrietta Branford
Jeff Brown
Keith Brumpton
June Crebbin
Helen Cresswell
Roald Dahl
Julia Donaldson

Anne Fine
Susan Gates
Pippa Goodhart
Douglas Hill
Mary Hoffman
Ann Jungman
Dick King-Smith
Robert Leeson
Penelope Lively

Jenny Nimmo
Alf Prøysen
Angie Sage
Jeremy Strong
Robert Swindells
Kaye Umansky
Jill Paton Walsh
Jacqueline Wilson

8-11

Richard Adams
Allan Ahlberg
Joan Aiken
Vivien Alcock
David Almond
Roy Apps
Lynne Reid Banks
J M Barrie
Frank L Baum
Lucy M Boston
Theresa Breslin
Keith Brumpton
Melvin Burgess
Lewis Carroll
Kathryn Cave
David Clement-Davies

Eoin Colfer
Susan Cooper
Bruce Coville
Helen Cresswell
Roald Dahl
Annie Dalton
Berlie Doherty
Edward Eager
Stephen Elboz
Penelope Farmer
Catherine Fisher
Nicholas Fisk
Pauline Fisk
Jostein Gaarder
Alan Garner
Susan Gates

Jamila Gavin
Alan Gibbons
Debi Gliori
Elizabeth Goudge
Kenneth Grahame
Diana Hendry
Nigel Hinton
Odo Hirsch
Russell Hoban
Michael Hoeye
Lesley Howarth
Ted Hughes
Eva Ibbotson
Brian Jacques
Tove Jansson
Robin Jarvis

Genres

8-11 (cont)

Paul Jennings
Diana Wynne Jones
Terry Jones
Ann Jungman
Garry Kilworth
Michael Lawrence
Robert Leeson
Gail Carson Levine
C S Lewis
Astrid Lindgren
Penelope Lively
Hugh Lofting
Lois Lowry
Geraldine McCaughrean
Cliff McNish
Andrew Matthews
William Mayne

Anne Merrick
Jill Murphy
Magdalen Nabb
E Nesbit
William Nicholson
Jenny Nimmo
Andrew Norriss
Mary Norton
Robert C O'Brien
Philippa Pearce
Ann Pilling
Stephen Potts
Terry Pratchett
Susan Price
Philip Pullman
Celia Rees
Enid Richemont

Philip Ridley
J K Rowling
Kate Saunders
Lemony Snicket
Paul Stewart
Catherine Storr
Alan Temperley
Kate Thompson
J R R Tolkien
Theresa Tomlinson
P L Travers
Ann Turnbull
Alison Uttley
Sylvia Waugh
E B White
T H White
Ursula Moray Williams

12-14

Joan Aiken
Vivien Alcock
Judy Allen
David Almond
K A Applegate
Natalie Babbitt
Steve Barlow and
     Steve Skidmore
Julie Bertagna
Theresa Breslin
Eoin Colfer
Louise Cooper
Susan Cooper
William Corlett
Annie Dalton
Peter Dickinson
Berlie Doherty
Stephen Elboz
Catherine Fisher

Jostein Gaarder (Philosophy)
Alan Garner
Susan Gates
Alan Gibbons
John Gordon
Virginia Hamilton
Diana Hendry
Nigel Hinton
Brian Jacques
Robin Jarvis
Pete Johnson
Diana Wynne Jones
Rhiannon Lassiter
Louise Lawrence
Ursula Le Guin
Lois Lowry
Geraldine McCaughrean
Catherine MacPhail
Margaret Mahy

Jan Mark
Stephen Moore
William Nicholson
Jenny Nimmo
Tamora Pierce
Terry Pratchett
Susan Price
Sally Prue
Philip Pullman
Philip Ridley
Katherine Roberts
J K Rowling
Lemony Snicket
Laura C Stevenson
Kate Thompson
J R R Tolkien
Sylvia Waugh

Genres

Friends

5-7

Rachel Anderson
Elizabeth Arnold
Brian Ball
Antonia Barber
Marc Brown
Lisa Bruce
Ann Cameron
Harriet Castor
Simon Cheshire
Michael Coleman
Gillian Cross
John Cunliffe

Lucy Daniels
Joyce Dunbar
Helen Dunmore
Dorothy Edwards
Anne Fine
Jamila Gavin
Elizabeth Hawkins
Tessa Krailing
Sheila Lavelle
Alan MacDonald
Hilary McKay
Marilyn McLaughlin

Jan Mark
Magdalen Nabb
Jenny Oldfield
Dyan Sheldon
Alexander McCall
   Smith
Emily Smith
Wendy Smith
Jean Ure
Bob Wilson
Selina Young

12-14

Keith Gray
Louis Sachar

Ghost/supernatural

5-7

Eleanor Allen
Judy Allen
Scoular Anderson
Tony Bradman
June Crebbin
Penny Dolan

Andrew Donkin
Alan Durant
Anne Fine
Sarah Garland
Sam Godwin
Anthony Masters

Barbara Mitchelhill
Catherine Sefton
Dee Shulman
Theresa Tomlinson
Jill Paton Walsh

8-11

Joan Aiken
Vivien Alcock
Mary Arrigan
Melvin Burgess
John Christopher
Sharon Creech
Jostein Gaarder
Grace Hallworth
Dennis Hamley
Douglas Hill
Eva Ibbotson
Julia Jarman
Pete Johnson

Allan Frewin Jones
Diana Wynne Jones
Ivan Jones
Robin Klein
Penelope Lively
Hilary McKay
Margaret Mahy
Jan Mark
Anthony Masters
Magdalen Nabb
Jenny Nimmo
Susan Price

Alison Prince
Maggie Prince
Celia Rees
Enid Richemont
Catherine Sefton
Paul Stewart
Catherine Storr
Robert Swindells
Kate Thompson
Jean Ure
Martin Waddell
Robert Westall

Ghost/supernatural (cont)

12-14

Joan Aiken
Vivien Alcock
David Almond
Peter Dickinson
Leon Garfield
Sandra Glover
John Gordon
Ann Halam

Eva Ibbotson
Paul Jennings
Pete Johnson
Penelope Lively
Margaret Mahy
Anthony Masters
Pat Moon

Jenny Nimmo
Susan Price
Celia Rees
Hugh Scott
Marcus Sedgwick
Sue Welford
Robert Westall

Historical

M Medieval • R Roman • T Tudor • V Victorian

5-7

Scoular Anderson
Roy Apps
Keith Brumpton
Rob Childs
Malachy Doyle

Mick Gowar
Dennis Hamley
Mary Hooper
Andrew Matthews
Michael Morpurgo

Margaret Nash
Karen Wallace
Jill Paton Walsh
Kirsty White
Philip Wooderson

8-11

Rachel Anderson
Roy Apps
Mary Arrigan
Antonia Barber
Theresa Breslin
Frances Hodgson
    Burnett V
Kevin Crossley-Holland M
Karen Cushman M

Terry Deary
Clive Dickinson
Berlie Doherty
Leon Garfield
Dennis Hamley V
Cynthia Harnett M
Mary Hooper
Anthony Horowitz
Julia Jarman

Terry Jones M
Geraldine McCaughrean
Michael Morpurgo
Alison Prince
Rosemary Sutcliff MR
Theresa Tomlinson
Ann Turnbull
Alison Uttley

12-14

Joan Aiken
Rachel Anderson
Gary Blackwood T
Henrietta Branford
Marita Conlon-McKenna
Susan Cooper T
Kevin Crossley-Holland
Karen Cushman M
Berlie Doherty
Leon Garfield
Susan Gates
Jamila Gavin

Adèle Geras
Dennis Hamley
Frances Mary Hendry
Catherine R Johnson
Julius Lester
Penelope Lively
Geraldine McCaughrean
Bel Mooney
Michael Morpurgo
Ruth Park V
Katherine Paterson

Gary Paulsen
Stephen Potts
Miriam Pressler
Alison Prince
Philip Pullman V
Celia Rees
Marcus Sedgwick
Rosemary Sutcliff
Mildred D Taylor
Theresa Tomlinson
Jill Paton Walsh

Genres

Horror

8-11

Nicholas Fisk
Allan Frewin Jones

Ann Pilling
R L Stine

12-14

Robert Cormier
Annie Dalton
Lois Duncan
Catherine Fisher

John Gordon
Ann Halam
Anthony Horowitz
Anthony Masters

Hugh Scott
Darren Shan
R L Stine

Humour

5-7

Allan Ahlberg
Jonathan Allen
Judy Allen
Scoular Anderson
Laurence Anholt
Roy Apps
Elizabeth Arnold
Alan Baron
Stan and Jan Berenstain
Claire Bevan
Terence Blacker
Adrian Boote
Tony Bradman
Herbie Brennan
Theresa Breslin
Joyce Lancaster Brisley
Marc Brown
Keith Brumpton
Janet Burchett and
    Sarah Vogler
Damon Burnard
Ann Cameron
Humphrey Carpenter
Anne Cassidy
Bennett Cerf
Simon Cheshire
Michael Coleman
June Crebbin
Helen Cresswell
John Cunliffe

Chris d'Lacey
Roald Dahl
Penny Dolan
Andrew Donkin
Malachy Doyle
Alan Durant
P D Eastman
Dorothy Edwards
Jonathan Emmett
Jan Fearnley
Vivian French
Sarah Garland
Susan Gates
Mick Gowar
Judy Hindley
Mary Hoffman
Mary Hooper
Rose Impey
Julia Jarman
Anita Jeram
Ann Jungman
Dick King-Smith
Sheila Lavelle
Theo Le Sieg
Robert Leeson
Penelope Lively
Arnold Lobel
Sam McBratney
Geraldine McCaughrean
Alan MacDonald

Marilyn McLaughlin
Colin McNaughton
Margaret Mahy
Jan Mark
James Marshall
Andrew and Paula Martyr
Anthony Masters
Kara May
Barbara Mitchelhill
Tony Mitton
Nicola Moon
Bel Mooney
Maggie Moore
Michaela Morgan
Jill Murphy
Margaret Nash
Jenny Oldfield
Hiawyn Oram
Jan Page
Brian Patten
Ann Pilling
Daniel Postgate
Jillian Powell
Chris Powling
Alison Prince
Alf Prøysen
Shoo Rayner
Alison Ritchie
Hilary Robinson
Frank Rodgers

Genres

Humour (cont)

5-7 (cont)

Phyllis Root
Michael Rosen
Margaret Ryan
Angie Sage
Catherine Sefton
Dr Seuss
Nick Sharratt
Dyan Sheldon
Dee Shulman
Francesca Simon

Alexander McCall Smith
Emily Smith
Wendy Smith
Paul Stewart
Jeremy Strong
Pat Thomson
Jill Tomlinson
Kaye Umansky
Martin Waddell

Barry Wade
Karen Wallace
Colin West
Ian Whybrow
Bob Wilson
David Henry Wilson
Jacqueline Wilson
Philip Wooderson
Selina Young

8-11

Allan Ahlberg
Laurence Anholt
Roy Apps
Philip Ardagh
Steve Barlow and
    Steve Skidmore
Julie Bertagna
Terence Blacker
Judy Blume
Henrietta Branford
Herbie Brennan
Theresa Breslin
Keith Brumpton
Anthony Buckeridge
Betsy Byars
Kathryn Cave
Simon Cheshire
Bruce Coville
Sharon Creech
Helen Cresswell
Richmal Crompton
Gillian Cross
Roald Dahl
Paula Danziger
Andrew Davies
Hunter Davies
Terry Deary
Clive Dickinson

Alan Durant
Anne Fine
Susan Gates
Morris Gleitzman
Debi Gliori
Mark Haddon
Willis Hall
Elizabeth Hawkins
Odo Hirsch
Michael Hoeye
Mary Hooper
Anthony Horowitz
Pat Hutchins
Eva Ibbotson
Rose Impey
Paul Jennings
Pete Johnson
Diana Wynne Jones
Ivan Jones
Ann Jungman
Jonathan Kebbe
Gene Kemp
Dick King-Smith
Robin Kingsland
Robin Klein
Sheila Lavelle
Michael Lawrence

Robert Leeson
Gail Carson Levine
Lois Lowry
Hilary McKay
Margaret Mahy
Jan Mark
Andrew Matthews
Jill Murphy
Andrew Norriss
Jenny Oldfield
Ann Pilling
Philip Ridley
Dyan Sheldon
Francesca Simon
E F Smith
Lemony Snicket
Angela Sommer-
    Bodenburg
Jeremy Strong
Alan Temperley
Hazel Townson
P L Travers
Kaye Umansky
Nicholas Warburton
Ian Whybrow
David Henry Wilson
Jacqueline Wilson

Genres

175

Humour (cont)

12-14

Ros Asquith
Steve Barlow and
   Steve Skidmore
Yvonne Coppard
Chris d'Lacey
Paula Danziger
Anne Fine
Morris Gleitzman

Elizabeth Honey
Cathy Hopkins
Anthony Horowitz
Eva Ibbotson
Paul Jennings
Hilary McKay
Terry Pratchett
Louise Rennison

Philip Ridley
Rosie Rushton
Louis Sachar
Moya Simons
Lemony Snicket
Sue Townsend
Jacqueline Wilson

Letters

5-7

Ian Whybrow

8-11

Herbie Brennan
Harry Horse
Helena Pielichaty
Jean Ure
Ian Whybrow

12-14

Judy Blume
Chris d'Lacey
Paula Danziger
Mary Hooper
Robert Leeson
Rosie Rushton

Magic

5-7

Jonathan Allen
Scoular Anderson
Roy Apps
Terence Blacker
Malorie Blackman
Humphrey Carpenter
Jonathan Emmett

Philippa Gregory
Julia Jarman
Ann Jungman
Sheila Lavelle
Andrew Matthews
Kara May
Jill Murphy

Jenny Nimmo
Jan Page
Alf Prøysen
Frank Rodgers
Catherine Sefton
Wendy Smith
Kaye Umansky

8-11

Edward Eager
Stephen Elboz
Jostein Gaarder
Debi Gliori
Douglas Hill

Diana Wynne Jones
Hilary McKay
Cliff McNish
Jill Murphy
Alf Prøysen

J K Rowling
Alan Temperley
P L Travers
Kaye Umansky

12-14

Annie Dalton
Stephen Elboz

Ursula Le Guin
Tamora Pierce

J K Rowling

Genres

176

Mythology

5-7
Pomme Clayton
Malachy Doyle
Jamila Gavin
Geraldine McCaughrean
Margaret Mahy
Margaret Mayo
Tony Mitton

8-11
Kevin Crossley-Holland
Ted Hughes
Terry Jones
Rosemary Sutcliff
T H White

12-14
Kevin Crossley-Holland
Robert Leeson
Katherine Roberts

Other cultures

5-7
Lisa Bruce
Jamila Gavin

8-11
Grace Hallworth
Gary Paulsen

12-14
Lynne Reid Banks
James Berry
Marita Conlon-McKenna
Farrukh Dhondy
Deborah Ellis
Nancy Farmer
Susan Gates
Virginia Hamilton

Frances Mary Hendry
Gaye Hiçyilmaz
Elizabeth Laird
Julius Lester
Elizabeth Lutzeier
Geraldine McCaughrean
Millie Murray
Miriam Pressler

Bali Rai
Stewart Ross
Suzanne Fisher Staples
Jean Ure
Cynthia Voigt
James Watson
Benjamin Zephaniah

Other lands

5-7
Malorie Blackman

8-11
Kate di Camillo
Mary Ellis
Jamila Gavin

Geraldine McCaughrean
Katherine Paterson

Gary Paulsen
Laura Ingalls Wilder

Genres

Other lands (cont)

12-14

Judy Allen
Lynne Reid Banks
James Berry
Anita Desai
Deborah Ellis
Kate Elizabeth Ernest

Elaine Forrestal
Paula Fox
Jamila Gavin
Jean Craighead George
Virginia Hamilton
Julius Lester

Beverley Naidoo
Suzanne Fisher Staples
Mildred D Taylor
Cynthia Voigt
Virginia Euwer Wolff

Pony/horse

5-7

Peter Clover
K M Peyton

8-11

Enid Bagnold
Wendy Douthwaite
Jenny Oldfield
K M Peyton
Anna Sewell

12-14

K M Peyton

Romance

8-11

Andrew Matthews

12-14

Ros Asquith
Veronica Bennett
Judy Blume
Robert Cormier
Chris d'Lacey
Paula Danziger
Helen Dunmore

Ruth Elwin Harris
Mary Hooper
Cathy Hopkins
Bel Mooney
K M Peyton
Chloë Rayban
Louise Rennison

Rosie Rushton
Dyan Sheldon
Jerry Spinelli
Jean Ure
Jacqueline Wilson
Virginia Euwer Wolff

School

5-7

Terence Blacker
Theresa Breslin
Humphrey Carpenter
Rob Childs
Michael Coleman
Gillian Cross
Susan Gates

Mick Gowar
Sheila Lavelle
Robert Leeson
Sam McBratney
Jan Mark
Margaret Nash

Jenny Oldfield
Dyan Sheldon
Francesca Simon
Pat Thomson
Jean Ure
Bob Wilson

Genres

School _(cont)

8-11

Allan Ahlberg
Bernard Ashley
Judy Blume
Enid Blyton
Tony Bradman
Elinor M Brent-Dyer
Anthony Buckeridge
Beverly Cleary
Richmal Crompton

Gillian Cross
Helen Dunmore
Anne Fine
Jack Gantos
Mary Hooper
Pat Hutchins
Jonathan Kebbe
Gene Kemp
Tessa Krailing

Robert Leeson
Jan Mark
William Mayne
Helena Pielichaty
J K Rowling
Russell Stannard
Jean Ure
Nicholas Warburton

12-14

Yinka Adebayo
Ros Asquith
Veronica Bennett
Gillian Cross

Josephine Feeney
Anne Fine
Jack Gantos
Michael Morpurgo

J K Rowling
Louis Sachar
Jerry Spinelli

Science fiction

5-7

Malorie Blackman
Douglas Hill

Sam McBratney
Paul Stewart

8-11

Rachel Anderson
Simon Cheshire
John Christopher
Bruce Coville
Terrance Dicks

Nicholas Fisk
Douglas Hill
Lesley Howarth
Jenny Nimmo

Andrew Norriss
Maggie Prince
Enid Richemont
Robert Swindells

12-14

Vivien Alcock
K A Applegate
Terence Blacker
Louise Cooper
Jamila Gavin
Margaret Haddix

Lesley Howarth
Rhiannon Lassiter
Louise Lawrence
Robert C O'Brien
Susan Price

Chloë Rayban
Gillian Rubinstein
Robert Swindells
Kate Thompson
Robert Westall

Social issues

8-11

Julie Bertagna
Malorie Blackman
Melvin Burgess
Chris d'Lacey
Jack Gantos

Alan Gibbons
Catherine MacPhail
Michael Morpurgo
Katherine Paterson
Gary Paulsen

Celia Rees
Ruth Symes
Theresa Tomlinson
Jacqueline Wilson

12-14

Yinka Adebayo
Judy Allen
David Almond
Rachel Anderson
Bernard Ashley
Lynne Reid Banks
Nina Bawden
Veronica Bennett
Julie Bertagna
Terence Blacker
Malorie Blackman
Judy Blume
Tim Bowler
Theresa Breslin
Melvin Burgess
Robert Cormier
Gillian Cross
Narinder Dhami
Farrukh Dhondy
Peter Dickinson
Berlie Doherty
Malachy Doyle
Alan Durant
Anne Fine
Elaine Forrestal
Paula Fox
Jack Gantos
Jamila Gavin

Adèle Geras
Alan Gibbons
Morris Gleitzman
Sandra Glover
Keith Gray
Rosa Guy
Carol Hedges
Gaye Hiçyilmaz
S E Hinton
Mary Hooper
Cathy Hopkins
Janni Howker
Angela Johnson
Catherine R Johnson
Pete Johnson
Julie Johnston
Brian Keaney
Elizabeth Laird
Robert Leeson
Joan Lingard
Elizabeth Lutzeier
Hilary McKay
Catherine MacPhail
Jan Mark
Sue Mayfield
Pat Moon
Bel Mooney

Michael Morpurgo
Millie Murray
Walter Dean Myers
Beverley Naidoo
Helena Pielichaty
Miriam Pressler
Sally Prue
Philip Pullman
Celia Rees
Philip Ridley
Malcolm Rose
Jacqueline Roy
Rosie Rushton
Louis Sachar
Dyan Sheldon
Nicky Singer
Sonya Sones
Jerry Spinelli
Robert Swindells
Jean Ure
Cynthia Voigt
Martin Waddell
James Watson
Sue Welford
Jacqueline Wilson
Virginia Euwer Wolff
Benjamin Zephaniah

Space

8-11

Mark Haddon
Russell Stannard
Sylvia Waugh

Genres

Sport

5-7

Janet Burchett and
  Sarah Vogler
Lindsay Camp

Rob Childs
Michael Coleman
Alan Durant

Alan MacDonald
Martin Waddell
Bob Wilson

8-11

Neil Arksey
Bernard Ashley
Terence Blacker
Tony Bradman
Rob Childs

Michael Coleman
Chris d'Lacey
Narinder Dhami
Alan Durant
Alan Gibbons

Michael Hardcastle
Paul May
Paul Stewart
Martin Waddell

12-14

Neil Arksey
Narinder Dhami

Alan Durant
Alan Gibbons

Stage

8-11

Antonia Barber
Noel Streatfeild

Thrillers

8-11

Helen Dunmore
Catherine Fisher

Pete Johnson
Robin Klein

Catherine MacPhail
K M Peyton

12-14

David Belbin
Malorie Blackman
Martin Booth
Melvin Burgess
Eoin Colfer
Robert Cormier
Gillian Cross
Lois Duncan
Alan Durant

Catherine Fisher
Margaret Haddix
Carol Hedges
Nigel Hinton
Anthony Horowitz
Lesley Howarth
Paul Jennings
Brian Keaney
Anthony Masters

K M Peyton
Philip Pullman
Celia Rees
Malcolm Rose
Robert Swindells
John Rowe Townsend
James Watson
Sue Welford

Traditional

5-7

Rose Impey
Andrew Matthews
Maggie Moore
Barry Wade

8-11

Kevin Crossley-Holland

War

WWI 1914-18 · WWII 1939-45

5-7

Jon Blake WWII
Dennis Hamley WWII
Robert Swindells WWII

8-11

Rachel Anderson WWII
Nina Bawden WWII
Andrew Davies WWII
Jackie French WWII
Adèle Geras WWII
Dennis Hamley
Elizabeth Hawkins WWII
Anne Holm WWII

Ann Jungman WWII
Judith Kerr WWII
Garry Kilworth
Robert Leeson WWII
Lois Lowry WWII
Michelle Magorian WWII
Michael Morpurgo WWII
Linda Newberry WWII

Alison Prince WWII
Maggie Prince WWII
Ian Serraillier WWII
Noel Streatfeild WWII
Robert Swindells WWII
Ann Turnbull WWII
Martin Waddell
Robert Westall WWII

12-14

Rachel Anderson
Bernard Ashley
Martin Booth WWI WWII
Theresa Breslin WWI
Marita Conlon-McKenna
   WWII
Deborah Ellis
Nancy Farmer
Ruth Elwin Harris WWI
Christa Laird WWII

Joan Lingard
Lois Lowry WWII
Elizabeth Lutzeier WWII
Michelle Magorian WWII
Michael Morpurgo WWII
Linda Newberry WWII
Robert C O'Brien
Gary Paulsen
Kit Pearson WWII
K M Peyton WWI

James Riordan WWII
Stewart Ross
Robert Swindells
Martin Waddell
Jill Paton Walsh WWII
Robert Westall WWII
Jane Yolen WWII
Benjamin Zephaniah

Genres

Series

This information is supplied by Peters Bookselling Services

Many children's books are published within series and this is often a helpful guide to finding similar authors.

Beginning to Read Series

Bodley Head Beginners
Beginner Books (Collins)
Bright and Early Books

Campbell Books
Classic Collection (Collins)

Disney's First Readers Levels 1/2/3

Early Step into Reading (US)

Fidgit and Quilly (Mike Haines)
First Storybooks

Giggle Club

I Am Reading
I Can Read (US)

Letterland Reading at Home
Little Kippers (Mick Inkpen)
Little Readers

My First I Can Read Books (US)

Orchard Toddler Books

Pat the Cat and Friends (Colin Hawkins)
Postman Pat Beginners (John Cunliffe)
Postman Pat Easy Readers (John Cunliffe)
Preston Pig (Colin McNaughton)

Read Aloud, Read Along, Read Alone (DK)
Read it Yourself
Reading Together (Walker)
Read Me: Beginners
Read with Ladybird: Levels 1/2/3
Read with Little Hippo
Ready, Steady, Read!
Red Fox Beginners
Red Nose Collection (Allan Ahlberg)
Red Nose Readers (Allan Ahlberg)

Share a Story

Thomas Easy to Read (Christopher Awdry)

Usborne Castle Tales
Usborne Farmyard Tales
Usborne Reading for Beginners
Usborne Rhyming Stories

Walker: Read Me

Easy Readers Series

A is for Amber (Paula Danziger)
Angels FC (Michael Coleman)
Animal Crackers (Rose Impey)

Beginner Books
Best Friends (Rosie Rushton)
Best Pets (Mary Hooper)
Blue Bananas
Bunch of Baddies (Andrew Matthews)

Cartwheels
Chillers
Collins Red Storybooks
Collins Yellow Storybooks

Colour Jets
Colour Young Puffin
Corgi Pups
Crackers
Crazy Gang (Nicola Matthews)
Creakie Hall (Karen Wallace)
Creepies

Dynamite Deela (Lisa Bruce)

Eek!

First Young Puffin
First Stepping Stone Books

Series

Fizzy (Michael Coleman)
Flying Foxes

Ginger Ninja (Shoo Rayner)
Glitter Girls (Caroline Plaisted)
Graffix

Happy Families (Allan Ahlberg)
Historical Storybooks
I Am Reading
I Can Read

Jets
Jumbo Jets

Kites

Leapfrog

Magic Tree House (Mary Pope Osborne)
Mona the Vampire (Sonia Holleyman)
Mr Majeika (Humphrey Carpenter)
Ms Wiz (Terence Blacker)
My First Read Alone

Orchard Crunchies
Orchard Fairy Tales
Orchard Super Crunchies

Pet Pals
Piccadilly Pips
Pleebus Books
Potbelly (Rose Impey)
Puffin Read Alone
Puzzle Planet Adventures

Read Alone (Hodder)
Read Me: Beginners
Read to Me Storybooks
Red Fox Ballet Books
Red Fox Beginners

Seriously Silly Stories (Laurence Anholt)
Share-a-story
Sheltie (Peter Clover)
Shivery Storybooks
Shooting Stars
Sparks
Sprinters
Starring Henrietta (Stan Cullimore)
Step into Reading (US)
Stepping Stone Books (US)
Super Stars

Tigers
Treetops
Tremors

Wizziwig (Geraldine McCaughrean)

Yellow Bananas
Young Corgi
Young Hippo
Young Hippo Adventure
Young Hippo Animal
Young Hippo Funny
Young Hippo Magic
Young Hippo School
Young Hippo Spooky
Young Puffin Read Alones

Novels

Series

Adventure! (Enid Blyton)
Adventure (Willard Price)
Adventures with Jeremy James
    (David Henry Wilson)
Anastasia (Lois Lowry)
Angels Unlimited (Annie Dalton)
Animal Alert (Jenny Oldfield)
Animal Ark (Lucy Daniels)
Animorphs (K A Applegate)
Are You Afraid of the Dark? (US)

Babysitters Club (Ann Martin)
Babysitters Mysteries (Ann Martin)
Ballerinas (Harriet Castor)

Ballet School (Emily Costello)
Bartlett (Odo Hirsch)
Bonechillers (B Haynes)

California Diaries (Ann Martin)
Chalet School (Elinor M Brent-Dyer)
Come and Have a Go ... (Haydn Middleton)
Comets
Comix
Crabtree Chronicles (Robin Kingsland)

Dragonslayer Academy (K H McMullan)
Dark Paths (Allan Frewin Jones)
Disney

Epix

Famous Five (Enid Blyton)
Flashbacks

Ghosts of Fear Street (R L Stine)
Give Yourself Goosebumps (R L Stine)
Goosebumps (R L Stine)
Glory Gardens (Bob Cattell)
Graffix
Graveyard School (Tom B Stone)

Happy Days (Enid Blyton)
Hardy Boys (Franklin W Dixon)
Harry Potter (J K Rowling)
Heartland (Lauren Brooke)
Hippo Adventure
Hippo Animal
Hippo Fantasy
Hippo Funny
Hippo Ghost
Hippo Mystery
Hippo Sport
Hollywell Stables (Samantha Alexander)
Home Farm Twins (Jenny Oldfield)
Hotshots (Terence Blacker)
How to Handle Your... (Roy Apps)

Internet Detectives (Michael Coleman)

Jackie (Judith M Berrisford)
Jennings (Anthony Buckeridge)
Jill (Ruby Ferguson)
Just William (Richmal Crompton)

Leggs United (Alan Durant)
Leopard Books (Scripture Union)
Little Terrors (Jan Burchett)

Mad Myths (Steve Barlow)
Mammoth Reads
Mammoth Storybooks
Magic Pony (Elizabeth Lindsay)
Midnight Dancer (Elizabeth Lindsay)
My Alien Classmate (Bruce Coville)
Mystery (Enid Blyton)

Nancy Drew (Carolyn Keene)
Newspaper Kids (Juanita Phillips)

Orchard Red Apples
Orchard Black Apples

Oxford Children's Modern Classics

Paddington Storybooks (Michael Bond)
Petsitters Club (Tessa Krailing)
Police Dog (Anthony Masters)
Puppy Patrol (Jenny Dale)
Puffin Classics
Puffin Modern Classics

Racers (Walker)
Riddles (Enid Blyton)
Riders (Samantha Alexander)

Saddle Club (Bonnie Bryant)
Sandy Lane Stables (Michelle Bates)
Secret Seven (Enid Blyton)
Series of Unfortunate Events
        (Lemony Snicket)
Seven Fabulous Wonders (Katherine Roberts)
Sister, Sister (US)
Sleepover Club
Soccer Mad (Rob Childs)
Spook Files (Michael Johnstone)
Spooksville (Christopher Pike)
Sprinters (Walker)
Stacey and Friends (Allan Frewin Jones)
Star Wars: Galaxy of Fear
Star wars: Young Jedi Knights
Stepping Stone Books (US)
Surfers
Sweet Valley Twins (Jamie Suzanne)
Sweet Valley Twins: Unicorn Club
                (Alice Nicole Johansson)
Sweet Valley Junior High (Jamie Suzanne)
Swoppers

The Blobheads (Paul Stewart)
The Edge Chronicles (Paul Stewart)
The Fab Four (Ros Asquith)
The Outfit (Robert Swindells)
The Web
The Zak Files (Dan Greenburg)
Tiger Books (Scripture Union)
Time Rangers (Rob Childs)
Total Football (Alan Gibbons)
Tudor Terror (Terry Deary)

Usborne Spinechillers

Walker Read Alones
Walker Story Books
We Love Animals (Jean Ure)
Weird World (Anthony Masters)

Series

Novels (cont)

Young Hippo
Young Hippo Adventure
Young Hippo Animal
Young Hippo Funny
Young Hippo Magic
Young Hippo School

Young Hippo Spooky
Young Hippo Sport
Young Puffin
Young Puffin Modern Classics
Young Puffin Storybooks

Young Adult Series

Angel

Blair Witch Files
Bondi Place (Jason Herbison)
Buffy the Vampire Slayer

Charmed
Circle of Three (Isobel Bird)
Confessions
Contents (Helen Flint)
Clueless

Dark Diary (Anthony Masters)
Dark Enchantment
Dawson's Creek (C J Anders)
Definitions
Discworld (Terry Pratchett)
Doctor Who

Fear Street
Fearless (Francine Pascal)

Hex (Rhiannon Lassiter)
His Dark Materials (Philip Pullman)
Hodder Fantasy
Hodder Science Fiction
Hodder Silver
Hodder Supernatural
Hodder Thrillers

J-17

Making Out (Katherine Applegate)
Making Waves (Katherine Applegate)
Mediator (Jenny Carroll)

Models (Chloë Rayban)
Mutant Point Horror

Night World (L J Smith)

Ocean City (Katherine Applegate)
Orchard Black Apple

Point
Point Crime
Point Fantasy
Point Horror
Point Horror Unleashed
Point Romance
Point Science Fiction

Replica (Marilyn Kaye)
Redwall (Brian Jacques)

Sabrina the Teenage Witch
Saga of Darren Shan (Darren Shan)
Signature
Star Trek
Star Wars
Step-chain (Ann Bryant)
Sugar Secrets
Suspense
Sweet Dreams
Sweet Valley High (Francine Pascal)
Sweet Valley University (John Laurie)

T·Witches (H B Gilmour)

What a Week to ... (Rosie Rushton)

X-Files

Series

Current Children's Book Prizes

This information on Prizes and Awards given for children's books has been supplied by Booktrust (formerly the National Book League), an independent educational charity. Much more book-related information may be obtained from the Booktrust website http://www.booktrusted.com

Hans Christian Andersen Awards
Biennial, presented in September

The highest international recognition given to authors and illustrators, these awards are presented to those whose complete works have made a lasting contribution to children's literature. The nominations are made by the national sections of IBBY, an international jury of children's literature specialists selects winners and the awards are presented during the biennial IBBY Congress in September or October. For further information contact: International Board on Books for Young People, Nonmenwag 12, Postfach CH-4003-Basel, Switzerland, tel: (+4161) 272 2917 email: ibby@eye.ch

	Author		Illustrator	
2002	Aidan Chambers	UK	Quentin Blake	UK
2000	Anna Maria Marchado	Brazil	Anthony Browne	UK
1998	Katherine Patterson	USA	Tomi Ungerer	France
1996	Uri Oriev	Israel	Klaus Eniskat	Germany

Angus Book Award
Announced in May

As an Angus-wide initiative to encourage pupils to read quality teenage fiction, from January to March, third year pupils read the five titles shortlisted by teachers and librarians from books written by UK resident authors and published in paperback in the preceding 12 months. The children discuss the books before they vote in a secret ballot. For further details, contact Jenni Amos, Press Officer, Angus Council, tel: 01307 473 049 email: amosj@angus.gov.uk

2002	*(Un)arranged Marriage*	Bali Rai	Corgi
2001	*Plague*	Malcolm Rose	Scholastic Point
2000	*Shadows*	Tim Bowler	Oxford University Press
1999	*River Boy*	Tim Bowler	Oxford University Press
1998	*Unbeliever*	Robert Swindells	Puffin

Askews Children's Book Award
Annual, announced in April

This new award aims to highlight quality fiction for 9 to 12 year olds, written by authors who have not already been shortlisted for major awards. The shortlist is selected by children's literature professionals and then children from Years 5, 6 and 7 are invited to vote for their favourite book from the shortlist, either by post or email: mail@askews.co.uk. For further details, contact: Rob Sanderson, Askews Children's Book Award, Askews Library Services Ltd, 218–222 North Road, Preston, Lancashire PR1 1SY, tel: 01772 490 489, email: roberts@askews.co.uk

2002	*(Un)arranged Marriage*	Bali Rai	Corgi

Prizes

Launched in 2000, the Blue Peter Book Awards are run by the BBC children's programme *Blue Peter* and awarded alongside the Reading Relay project being run by public libraries throughout the UK. There are two main sections to these awards: The Judges' Awards and The Voters' Awards. For the Judges' Awards, a celebrity judging panel selects the shortlists from paperback titles published in the UK in the previous year. These books are then read by Blue Peter Young Judges chosen as a result of a Blue Peter Book Review Competition. They chose the winners for each of three categories. From these three winning titles, a Book of the Year is selected. The Voters' Awards are voted for by children across the UK via their local library. For further information contact: Scottish Book Trust, 137 Dundee Street, Edinburgh EH11 1BG, tel: 0131 229 3663 or fax: 0131 228 4293, website: www.scottishbooktrust.com. Alternatively, visit the Blue Peter Book Award website: www.bbc.co.uk/cbbc/bluepeter/books/index.shtml

2002 The Judges' Awards

The Book I Couldn't Put Down and The Blue Peter 2002 Book of the Year Award
Feather Boy   Nicky Singer   Collins

The Best Book to Read Aloud
Crispin, the Pig Who Had It All   Ted Dewan   Random House

The Best New Information Book
The Computer Wizard of Victorian England Lucy Lethbridge   Short Books

2002 The Voters' Awards
The Best Storybook
Tracy Beaker   Jacqueline Wilson   Transworld
                                                 illus. by Nick Sharratt

The Best Book with Facts
The Terrible Tudors   Terry Deary & Neil Tonge   Scholastic

2001 The Judges' Awards
The Best Book to Keep Forever   Oxford
The Kite Rider   Geraldine McCaughrean   University Press

The Book I Couldn't Put Down and The Blue Peter 2001 Book of the Year Award
The Wind Singer   William Nicholson   Egmont

The Best Book to Read Aloud
The Bravest Ever Bear   Allan Ahlberg   Walker
                                                 illus. by Paul Howard

2001 The Voters' Awards
The Best Storybook
Harry Potter and the Philosopher's Stone   J K Rowling   Bloomsbury

The Best Book of Knowledge
Rotten Romans   Terry Deary   Scholastic

2000 The Judges' Awards
A Special Book to Keep Forever and The Blue Peter 2000 Book of the Year Award
A Pilgrim's Progress   Retold by Geraldine McCaughrean   Hodder
                                                 illus. by Jason Cockroft

The Book I Couldn't Put Down
Shadow of the Minotaur   Alan Gibbons   Orion

The Best Book to Read Aloud
The Gruffalo   Julia Donaldson   Macmillan
                                                 illus. by Axel Scheffler

Prizes

Blue Peter Children's Book Awards (cont)

2000 The Voters' Awards
The Best Book With Facts
Guinness World Records   Guinness

The Book that Made Me Laugh the Loudest
Matilda   Roald Dahl   Puffin
                                       illus. by **Quentin Blake**

The Best Book to Share
Harry Potter and the Goblet of Fire J K Rowling   Bloomsbury

Branford Boase Award Annual, presented in June/July

This award began in 2000 and is in memory of two very important figures in the children's book world, both of whom died of cancer in 1999. Henrietta Branford was a talented, award-winning children's novelist and Wendy Boase was a passionate children's book editor who was the Editorial Director of Walker Books as well as being one of its founders. Supported by several publishers, headed by Walker Books, this annual prize is awarded to an outstanding first-time novel for children and is usually presented in June/July. For further details, contact the administrator Gerry Etherington, tel: 023 8055 5057, email: locol@compuserve.com

2001 *Floodland*   Marcus Sedgwick   Orion Children's Books
2000 *Song Quest*   Katherine Roberts   Orion Children's Books

Caldecott Medal Annual, announced January/February

Instituted in 1938 and named after the English illustrator Randolph Caldecott (1846–1886), this award is presented for the most distinguished American picture book for children published in the preceding year

2002 *The Three Pigs*   David Weisner   Clarion/Houghton Mifflin
2001 *So You Want to Be President*   Text: Judith St George   Philomel Books, USA
                                          Illus. by David Small
2000 *Joseph Had a Little Overcoat* Simms Taback   Viking Children's Books, USA
1999 *Snowflake Bentley*   Jacqueline Briggs Martin Houghton Mifflin
                                          Illus. by Mary Azarian
1998 *Rapunzel*   Paul O Zelinsky   Dutton Children's Books

Carnegie and Greenaway Awards

The Carnegie and Kate Greenaway awards are presented annually by CILIP and administered by the Youth Libraries Group of CILIP. Nominations are submitted by institute members and winners selected by a panel of 13 children's librarians.

Carnegie Medal Annual, announced in July

Instituted in 1936, the Carnegie Medal is given for an outstanding book for children. Contenders are appraised for characterisation, plot, style, accuracy, imaginative quality and that indefinable element that lifts the book above the others. The date of the award is based on the date that the books were published, not when the award is announced. Administered by: CILIP, 7 Ridgmount Street, London WC1E 7AE, tel: 020 7255 0650, fax: 020 7255 0501, email: marketing@la-hq.org.uk

2001 *The Amazing Maurice and   Terry Pratchett   Doubleday
           His Educated Rodents*
2000 *The Other Side of Truth*   Beverley Naidoo   Puffin
1999 *Postcards From No Man's Land* Aidan Chambers   The Bodley Head
1998 *Skellig*   David Almond   Hodder Children's Books
1997 *River Boy*   Tom Bowler   Oxford University Press

Prizes

This is awarded to the best work of fiction published in the year preceding the year of the award. There are three category winners: Books for Younger Children (previously 'picture book'); Books for Younger Readers (previously 'shorter novel'); and Books for Older Readers (previously 'longer novel'), and an overall winner. The winner is chosen by nominations from children throughout the UK - entries are not required. For more information, contact the Administrator, The Federation of Children's Book Groups, c/o Marianne Adey, Co-ordinator, The Old Malt House, Aldbourne, Marlborough, Wiltshire SN8 2DW, tel: 01672 540629 or fax 01672 541280, alternatively visit www.fcbg.org.uk or email marianneadey@aol.com

2002 Books for Younger Children
The Man Who Wore All His Clothes — Allan Ahlberg, illus. by Katherine McEwen — Walker

Books for Younger Readers
Out of the Ashes — Michael Morpurgo, illus. by Michael Foreman — Macmillan

Books for Older Readers and 2002 Overall Winner
Noughts and Crosses — Malorie Blackman — Doubleday

2001 Picture Book and 2001 Overall Winner
Eat Your Peas — Kes Gray, illus. by Nick Sharratt — The Bodley Head

Shorter Novel
Lizzie Zipmouth — Jacqueline Wilson, illus. by Nick Sharratt — Corgi

Longer Novel
Harry Potter and the Goblet of Fire — J K Rowling — Bloomsbury

2000 Picture Book
Demon Teddy — Nicholas Allan, illus. by Nicholas Allan — Hutchinson

Shorter Novel and 2000 Overall Winner
Kensuke's Kingdom — Michael Morpurgo, illus. by Michael Foreman — Heinemann

Longer Novel
Harry Potter and the Prisoner of Azkaban — J K Rowling — Bloomsbury

1999 Picture Book
What! — Kate Lum, illus. by Adrian Johnson — Bloomsbury

Shorter Novel
Little Dad — Pat Moon, illus. by Nick Sharratt — Mammoth

Longer Novel and 1999 Overall Winner
Harry Potter and the Chamber of Secrets — J K Rowling — Bloomsbury

1998 Picture Book
The Lion Who Wanted to Love — Giles Andreae, illus. by Giles Andreae — Orchard

Shorter Novel
Nightmare Stairs — Robert Swindells — Doubleday

Longer Novel and 1998 Overall Winner
Harry Potter and the Philosopher's Stone — J K Rowling — Bloomsbury

Prizes

Children's Laureate

The Children's Laureate is chosen every two years and is somebody who writes or illustrates books that young people love. Their books are the kind that you'll never give away, books you'll remember for the rest of your life. The Children's Laureate is a working prize intended to provide a platform for the winner to stimulate public discussion about the importance of children's literature and reading in a forward looking society. Administration is by the British section of the International Board on Books for Young People (IBBY). The first Children's Laureate was Quentin Blake (1999-2001) and the second is Anne Fine (2001-2003). A new Children's Laureate will be named in May 2003.

Fidler Award

This prize is awarded to a previously unpublished author for a novel aimed at eight to twelve year-olds and is an advance of £1,500, a royalty package, a silver and rosewood trophy (to be held for one year) and publication by Hodder Children's Books. Kathleen Fidler was the author of over 80 books for children, many of which were broadcast on BBC Radio Children's Hour and Schools programmes. She had a long-standing affection for Scotland and, over the years, worked closely with the Edinburgh Children's Book Group. After her death in 1980, the members of that group, together with her publishers, Blackie & Son Ltd, and Mary Baxter, then Chief Executive of the National Book League in Scotland (now Scottish Book Trust), established the Kathleen Fidler Award as a memorial to her deep interest in children and writers. In 1996, Hodder Children's Books took over the sponsorship of the award and the name was changed to the Fidler award. For further information contact: Scottish Book Trust, 137 Dundee Street, Edinburgh EH11 1BG, tel: 0131 229 3663 or fax 0131 228 4293, website: www.scottishbooktrust.com

2001	The Ice Boy	Patricia Elliott
2000	The Ivy Crown	Gill Vickery
1999	The Memory Prisoner	Thomas Bloor
1998	No award	
1997	Slate Mountain	Mark Leyland

The Kate Greenaway Medal

This award was instituted in 1955 and goes to an artist who has produced the most distinguished work in the illustration of children's books. Nominated books are assessed for design, format and production as well as artistic merit and must have been published in the UK during the previous year. Administered by: CILIP, 7 Ridgmount Street, London WC1E 7AE, tel: 020 7255 0650, fax: 020 7255 0501, email: marketing@la-hq.org.uk

2001	Chris Riddell	Pirate Diary: The Journal of Jake Carpenter [written by Richard Platt]	Walker
2000	Lauren Child	I Will Not Ever Never Eat a Tomato [written by Lauren Child]	Walker
1999	Helen Oxenbury	Alice's Adventures in Wonderland [written by Lewis Carroll]	Walker
1998	Helen Cooper	Pumpkin Soup [written by Helen Cooper]	Doubleday
1997	P J Lynch	When Jessie Came Across the Sea [written by Amy Hest]	Walker

Prizes

Guardian Children's Fiction Award
Annual, announced in September

The prize of £1,500 is awarded to an outstanding work of fiction for children (not picture books) written by a British or Commonwealth author and first published in the UK during the calendar year preceding the year in which the award is presented. Following publisher entry only, the winner is chosen by a panel of authors and the review editor for The Guardian's Children's Books section. For more information contact *The Guardian* Newspaper, 119 Farringdon Road, London EC1R 3ER, tel: 020 7239 9694 or fax: 020 8713 4366, alternatively, visit the website.

Year	Title	Author	Publisher
2002	*Thursday's Child*	Sonya Hartnett	Walker
2001	*The Seeing Stone*	Kevin Crossley-Holland	Orion
2000	*The Illustrated Mum*	Jacqueline Wilson	Transworld
1999	*The Sterkarm Handshake*	Susan Price	Scholastic
1998	*Fire, Bed and Bone*	Henrietta Branford	Walker
1997	*Junk*	Melvin Burgess	Penguin

Lancashire County Library Children's Book of the Year
Annual, announced in June

The prize of £500 and an engraved decanter is awarded to the best work of fiction for 12 to 14 year-olds, written by a UK author and first published between 1 September and 31 August of the previous year. Publishers submit books for consideration and the winner is chosen by the County's secondary-school pupils. For more information, contact Jean Wolstenholme, tel: 01772 264 040 or fax: 01772 264 043, email: library@lcl.lancscc.gov.uk

Year	Title	Author	Publisher
2002	*Noughts and Crosses*	Malorie Blackman	Doubleday
2001	*Bloodtide*	Melvin Burgess	Puffin
	Plague	Malcolm Rose	Scholastic Point
2000	*Shadows*	Tim Bowler	Oxford University Press
1999	*Out of Darkness*	Nigel Hinton	Puffin
1998	*Jay*	Elizabeth Hawkins	Orchard

NASEN Special Needs Book Award
Annual, announced in November

This award is sponsored by the National Association for Special Educational Needs and the Educational Publishers Council. The award, a prize of £500, is given to the book of any genre that most successfully provides a positive image of children or young people with special needs. The judges look for books that are well written and well presented and which can be appreciated by all children under the age of 16, not just those with special needs. Administered by: The Publishers Association, 1 Kingsway, London WC2B 6XF, tel: 020 7565 7474, fax: 020 7836 4543, website: www.publishers.org.uk

Year	Title	Author	Publisher
2002	*Running on Empty*	Anna Paterson	Lucky Duck
2001	*Joey Pigza Swallowed the Key*	Jack Gantos	Corgi Yearling
2000	*Susan Laughs*	Jeanne Willis and Tony Ross	Anderson Press
1999	*Sweet Clarinet*	James Riorden	Oxford University Press
1998	*The Crowstarver*	Dick King-Smith	Doubleday
1997	*Charlie's Eye*	Dorothy Horgan	Hamish Hamilton

Prizes

The Nestlé Smarties Book Prize was established to encourage high standards and stimulate interest in books for children. Eligible books are those written in English by an author who is a citizen of or resident in the United Kingdom and who is living at the time the book is published. Gold, Silver and Bronze awards are given in each of three categories: 5 and under, 6 to 8 and 9 to 11 years. Since 1996, the winners have been selected by young judges from a short-list drawn up by adult judges. For enquiries about the prize please contact: Tarryn McKay, Booktrust, Book House, 45 East Hill, London SW18 2QZ, tel: 020 8516 2972.

2002 Gold Awards

9-11	Mortal Engines	Philip Reeve	Scholastic
6-8	That Pesky Rat	Lauren Child	Orchard
5 & under	Jazzy in the Jungle	Lucy Collins	Walker

2001 Gold Awards

9-11	Journey to the River Sea	Eva Ibbotson	Macmillan
6-8	The Shrimp	Emily Smith	Young Corgi
5 & under	Chimp and Zee	Catherine and Laurence Anholt	Frances Lincoln

2000 Gold Awards

9-11	The Wind Singer	William Nicholson	Mammoth
6-8	Lizzie Zipmouth	Jacqueline Wilson	Young Corgi
5 & under	Max	Bob Graham	Walker

1999 Gold Awards

9-11	Harry Potter and the Prisoner of Azkaban	J K Rowling	Bloomsbury
6-8	Snow White and the Seven Aliens	Laurence Anholt illus. by Arthur Robbins	Orchard
5 & under	The Gruffalo	Julia Donaldson illus. by Axel Scheffler	Macmillan

1998 Gold Awards

9-11	Harry Potter and the Chamber of Secrets	J K Rowling	Bloomsbury
6-8	The Last Gold Diggers	Harry Horse	Puffin Books
5 & under	Cowboy Baby	Sue Heap	Walker

1997 Gold Awards

9-11	Harry Potter and the Philosopher's Stone	J K Rowling	Bloomsbury
6-8	The Owl Tree	Jenny Nimmo	Walker
5 & under	Leon and Bob	Simon James	Walker

This award is named after John Newbery (1713-1767), a London bookseller and first publisher of children's books. It was instituted in 1922 and is the most important American award given annually for the most distinguished contribution to American literature for children published in the previous year. The recipient must be resident in or a citizen of the United States. For further details, contact the Association for Library Services to Children at the American Library Association, 50 East Huron Street, Chicago, IL 70711-2795 USA, tel: +1 312 280 2163, fax: +1 312 280 3257.

2002	A Single Shard	Linda Sue Park	Clarion/Houghton Mifflin
2001	A Year Down Yonder	Richard Peck	Dial Books for young Readers
2000	Bud, Not Buddy	Christopher Paul Curtis	Delacourte
1999	Holes	Louis Sachar	Farrar, Straus & Giroux UK: Bloomsbury
1998	Out of the Dust	Karen Hesse	Scholastic

Prizes

Initiated in 1999, this prize is awarded to a book written by an author resident in the UK and first published in paperback between April one year and April the next. A shortlist of five titles is selected by local librarians and teachers in conjunction with Northumberland Schools Library Service and the final winner is chosen by Year 10 pupils from participating schools. For more information, contact: Eileen Armstrong, Cramlington High School, Cramlington, Northumberland NE23 6BN, tel: 01670 712 311, fax: 01670 730 598.

2002	*Blue*	Sue Mayfield	Hodder Children's Books
2001	*Hard Man of the Swings*	Jeanne Willis	Faber
2000	*Megan*	Mary Hooper	Bloomsbury
1999	*Harry Potter and the Chamber of Secrets*	J K Rowling	Bloomsbury

Sheffield Children's Book Award

The Sheffield Children's Book Award began in 1989 and is presented annually to the book chosen as the most enjoyable by the children of Sheffield. The majority of the judges look at, read and vote on the shortlisted books within their class at school. There are three category winners and an overall winner. For further details contact: Jennifer Wilson (Book Award Co-ordinator), c/o Schools Library Service Sheffield, tel: 0114 250 6843, email: bookaward@dial.pipex.com

2000 Picture Book
Harry and the Bucketful of Dinosaurs Ian Whybrow David and Charles
illus. by Adrian Reynolds Children's Books

Shorter Novel and 2000 Overall Winner
Cry Wolf Susan Gates Scholastic
Longer Novel
Harry Potter and the Prisoner of Azkaban J K Rowling Bloomsbury

1999 Picture Book
The Time it Took Tom Nick Sharratt Scholastic
and Stephen Tucker Children's Books

Shorter Novel
Buried Alive Jacqueline Wilson Yearling
illus. by Nick Sharratt and Sue Heap

Longer Novel and 1999 Overall Winner
Abomination Robert Swindells Yearling

1998 6 and under
Mucky Pup Ken Brown Anderson Press
7-11
Pirate Pandemonium Jeremy Strong A & C Black
illus. by Judy Brown

12 and over and 1998 Overall Winner
Harry Potter and the Philosopher's Stone J K Rowling Bloomsbury

1997 6 and under and 1997 Overall Winner
A Cheese and Tomato Spider Nick Sharratt Andre Deutsch
7-11
Bad Girls Jacqueline Wilson Corgi Yearling
illus. by Judy Brown

12 and over
Death or Glory Boys Theresa Breslin Mammoth Books

1996 6 and under
The Last Noo-noo Jill Murphy Walker
7-11 and 1996 Overall Winner
Double act Jacqueline Wilson Doubleday
illus. by Nick Sharratt and Sue Heap

12 and over
Unbeliever Robert Swindells Hamish Hamilton

Prizes

South Lanarkshire Book Award

Books published in paperback in Britain between September 2000 and August 2001 were eligible for the 2002 Award. A panel of School Librarians, Area Librarians and the Literacy Development Co-ordinator chose the four shortlisted titles. Groups of S3 pupils (14 to 15 year-olds) from 8 schools in South Lanarkshire read the shortlisted titles, and voted for the winner, which was announced on Monday 18 March 2002. For more details contact: Margaret Cowan, Literacy Development Co-ordinator, Central Library, 40 The Olympia, East Kilbride G74 1PG, tel: 01355 248 581, fax: 01355 229 365.

2002	*Storm Catchers*	Tim Bowler	Oxford University Press
2001	*Missing*	Catherine MacPhail	Bloomsbury

Tir na n-Og Award

The Tir na n-Og Awards are three prizes of £1000 awarded annually to acknowledge the work of authors and illustrators in three categories. These are Best Fiction of the Year (original Welsh-language novels, stories and picture-books are considered); Best Welsh-Language Non-fiction Book of the Year; and Best English (Anglo-Welsh) Book of the Year (with an authentic Welsh background, fiction and non-fiction). Books must be published during the preceding year. For more details, contact the Administrators: Welsh Books Council, Castell Brychan, Aberystwyth SY23 2JB, tel: 01970 624 151 or fax: 01970 625 385, email: castellbrychan@cllc.org.uk, website: www.cllc.org.uk

2002	Best Welsh Fiction		
	Gwirioni	Shoned Wyn Jones	Y Lolfa
	Best Welsh Non-fiction		
	Poeth!	Editor Non Ap Emlyn Designer Marian Delyth	Y Lolfa
	Best English Fiction		
	Georgie	Malachy Doyle	Bloomsbury
2001	Best Welsh Fiction		
	Llinyn Trôns	Bethan Gwanas	Y Lolfa
	Best Welsh Non-fiction		
	Myrddin ap Dafydd	Jan Coch Mewn Pwdin Reis	Hughes
	Best English Fiction		
	Arthur: The Seeing Stone	Kevin Crossley-Holland	Orion
2000	Best Welsh Fiction		
	Ta-Ta Tryweryn	Gwenno Hughes	Gomer
	Best Welsh Non-fiction		
	Chwedlau o 'r Gwledydd Celtaidd	Rhiannon Ifans and Margaret Jones	Y Lolfa
	Best English Fiction		
	Artworks on ... Interiors	Jo Dahn and Justin Baldwin	FBA Publications
1999	Best Welsh Fiction		
	Pam Fi Eto, Duw?	John Owen	Y Lolfa
	Best Welsh Non-fiction		
	Byw a Bod yn y Bàth	Lis Jones	Gwasg Carreg Gwalch
	Best English Fiction		
	Rhian's Song	Gillian Drake	Pont/Gomer Press

Prizes

1998	Best Welsh Fiction		
	Dyddiau Cwn	Gwen Redvers Jones	Gomer
	Best Welsh Non-fiction		
	Stori Branwen	Tegwin Jones and Jac Jones	Gomer
	Best English Fiction		
	Alwena's Garden	Mary Oldham	Pont Books
1997	Best Welsh Fiction		
	Ydy Fe!	John Owen	Iaith Cyf
	Best Welsh Non-fiction		
	Dirgelwch Loch Ness	Gareth F Williams	Y Lolfa
	Best English Fiction		
	Cities in the Sea	Sian Lewis	Pont Gomer
		Illus. by Jackie Morris	

Whitbread Children's Book of the Year Award   Annual, announced in January

The Whitbread awards started in 1971 and the first award for a children's novel was given in 1972. The format changed in 1985 when the Whitbread Book of the Year was launched, and in 1996, children's books were taken out of the main category and given a prize of their own. Entries must be by authors who have been resident in the UK or Eire for three years and whose book has been published between 1 November and 31 October of the year of the prize. The prize is £5,000. The winner is announced in January. 1999 was the first year the winner of the Whitbread Children's Book of the Year Award was also considered for the overall Whitbread Book of the Year Award, with a prize of £25,000. Main contact: Sunita Rappai, Karen Earl Ltd, 66 Great Suffolk Street, London SE1 0BL, tel: 020 7202 2822, fax: 020 7202 2802, email: sunita@karen-earl.co.uk

2002	*Saffy's Angel*	Hilary McKay	Hodder Children's Books
2001	*The Amber Spyglass*	Philip Pullman	Scholastic
2000	*Coram Boy*	Jamilla Gavin	Mammoth
1999	*Harry Potter and the Prisoner of Azkaban*	J K Rowling	Bloomsbury
1998	*Skellig*	David Almond	Hodder Children's Books
1997	*Aquilla*	Andrew Norriss	Puffin

Wirral Paperback of the Year   Annual, announced in July/August

Set up in 1995, this award is organised by the Wirral Schools Library Service. It aims to give young people from the area the chance to read exciting new fiction. The Schools Library Service chooses 20 titles, first published in paperback in the preceding year. Copies are lent to up to 20 local secondary schools. Year 8 and 9 pupils from each school choose their own shortlist and a Wirral shortlist is then compiled from these in May. Representatives from each school meet in July to discuss and vote for their favourite book. For further information contact: Mary Bryning, Wirral Schools Library Service, Wirral Education Centre, Acre Lane, Bromborough, Wirral CH62 7BZ, tel: 0151 346 1184, email: sls@wirral.gov.uk

2002	*Stormbreaker*	Anthony Horowitz	Walker
2001	*Holes*	Louis Sachar	Bloomsbury
	The Raging Quiet	Sherryl Jordan	Simon & Schuster
2000	*Face*	Benjamin Zephaniah	Bloomsbury
1999	*Pig-heart Boy*	Malorie Blackman	Young Corgi
1998	*The Tulip Touch*	Anne Fine	Puffin
1997	*The Shadow of August*	Sue Welford	Oxford University Press

Prizes

Bibliography

There are many specialist reference books and periodicals which provide information on children's authors. The following list highlights some that you may find especially useful. They should be available through your local library.

Books

- *Children's Fiction Index* 7th Ed 1993
  Edited by Jennifer Malden and Margaret Hobson
  ISBN 0 900092 85 8
  Association of Assistant Librarians

- *Children's Fiction Sourcebook:* 2nd Ed 1995
  A Survey of Children's Books for 6-13 Year Olds
  Edited by Margaret Hobson and Jennifer Malden
  ISBN 1 85928 083 8
  Scolar Press, Ashgate Publishing

- *Children's Sequels* 9th Ed 1999
  Edited by Margaret Hobson
  Library Association

- *Oxford Companion to Children's Literature* 1999
  Edited by Humphrey Carpenter and Mari Prichard
  ISBN 0 19 860228 6
  Oxford University Press

- *The Cambridge Guide to Children's Books in English* 2001
  Edited by Victor Watson
  ISBN 0 521 55064 5
  Cambridge University Press

- *Twentieth Century Children's Writers* 3rd Ed 1989
  ISBN 0 912289 95 3
  St James Press (USA)

- *100 Best Books: Books for up to 16 Year Olds* 2002
  Published each year
  Young Book Trust

- *The Rough Guide to Children's Books 5-11 Years* 2002
  Nicholas Tucker
  ISBN 1 85828 788 X
  Rough Guides

- *The Rough Guide to Children's Books 0-5 Years* 2002
  Nicholas Tucker
  ISBN 1 85828 787 1
  Rough Guides

- *A Multicultural Guide to Children's Books, 0-16* 1999
  Compiled by Judith Elkin, edited by Rosemary Stones
  ISBN 1 871566 05 3
  Co-published by Books for Keeps and the Reading & Language
  Information Centre, University of Reading

Books (cont)

- *Hadithi Nzuri: A Good Story*
  Children's literature from Africa, Asia and Latin America
  Compiled and written by Taahra Ghazi
  Actionaid

- *Children's Literature*   2001
  Peter Hunt
  ISBN 0 631 21141 1
  Blackwell

- *Son of Invisible Art: Graphic Novels for Libraries*   2001
  Compiled by Joss O'Kelly
  ISBN 0 86059 605 2
  Buckinghamshire County Library

Periodicals

- *Books for Keeps: The Children's Book Magazine*
  Books for Keeps
  6 Brightfield Road, Lee
  London SE12 8QF
  Phone: 020 8852 4953
  E-mail: booksforkeeps@btinternet.com
  Six issues per year

- *Carousel: The Guide to Children's Books*
  Carousel
  The Saturn Centre
  54–76 Bissell Street
  Birmingham B5 7HX
  Phone: 0121 622 7458
  E-mail: carousel.guide@virgin.net
  Three issues per year plus Christmas supplement

- *The School Librarian*
  School Library Association
  4 Llys Cerrig
  St Asaph LL17 0BZ
  Cornwall
  Phone: 01745 730203
  E-mail: rel@aber.ac.uk
  Four issues per year

Websites

Of the many websites that have been looked into, the one which provides the most useful set of book-related information is administered by Booktrust, an educational charity supported by most authors, publishers and other information providers. The site address is www.booktrusted.com

Other sites that are current and helpful include:
www.achuka.co.uk
www.cool-reads.co.uk
www.mrsmad.com

Index

Index

Author	Age ranges	Page numbers

Index

Index

Index

203

Author	Age ranges	Page numbers

Index

Index

Index

Norah Irvin is a qualified librarian, with many years' experience of working with children and young people, in schools and in the public libraries of Hertfordshire.

Her career with Hertfordshire Library Service and Hertfordshire Schools Library Service has provided her with the opportunity to:

- formulate book selection policy for the county
- advise schools on library and book provision
- advise parent/teacher groups on reading
- select stock for schools and Schools Library Service centres
- run courses for teachers on using books with children
- give book talks in both schools and public libraries

When working as Promotion and Marketing Co-ordinator for Hertfordshire Library Service, Norah was responsible for the development in Hertfordshire of *Bookstart*. Designed 'to bring books to babies' through health centres, the project also included a video to alert parents to the importance of using books with very young children. She was also involved in the organisation of Hertfordshire's literature festival for three years and introduced the children's book element to it.

Fourth edition of a
standard reference and
reading promotion work

The essential tool for all
who read adult fiction

ISBN 1 901786 57 9
£17.99

Available from

Library & Information Statistics Unit (LISU)
Loughborough University
LOUGHBOROUGH
Leics
LE11 3TU

Tel +44 (0)1509 223071   Fax + 44 (0)1509 223072   Email lisu@lboro.ac.uk